Official Know-It-All Guide™

LET'S GET RESULTS, NOT EXCUSES!

James M. Bleech
Dr. David G. Mutchler

Frederick Fell Publishers, Inc.
2131 Hollywood Blvd., Suite 305, Hollywood, FL 33020
Phone: (954) 925-5242   Fax: (954) 925-5244
Web Site: www.Fellpub.com

Fell's Official Know-It-All Guide

Frederick Fell Publishers, Inc.

2131 Hollywood Boulevard, Suite 305

Hollywood, Florida 33020

954-925-5242

e-mail: fellpub@aol.com

Visit our Web site at www.fellpub.com

Library of Congress Cataloging in Publication Data

Bleech, James M., 1948-

    Let's get results, not excuses! : a leader's guide to effecting change in corporate America / by James M. Bleech and David G. Mutchler.

      p. cm.
    Originally published: Grand Rapids, MI : MBP Press, c1994.
    Includes bibliographical references (p.243)
    ISBN 0-88391-070-5
    1. Organizational change. 2. Leadership 3. Excuses.
    I. Mutchler, David G., 1942- II. Title.
    HD58.8.B57   1995, 2002   95-188
    658.4' 063--dc20   CIP

10 9 8 7 6 5 4 3 2

Editorial by: Oleg Alexander
Graphic Design by: Elena Solis

Excerpts From Articles About
Let's Get Results, Not Excuses!

by James M. Bleech and David G. Mutchler

"Many CEOs spend all day chasing excuses. Instead they should be working to create an excuse-free culture."

(source) The Wall Street Journal

"The proper preparation or planning by management will eliminate excuses before they can be used."

(source) Chicago Tribune

"If your shop's productivity suffers because employees routinely make excuses for not getting the job done, you're not alone. Employees' excuse-making is one of the biggest challenges in business."

(source) Nation's Business

"The many excuses employees give for work not done or not done well diminishes the organization's productivity and thus affects the company's bottom line."

(source) The Denver Post

Comments About
Let's Get Results, Not Excuses!

by James M. Bleech and David G. Mutchler

"So simple and seemingly so obvious, but a 'real awakening' to me. Extremely insightful as to the true value of eliminating excuses in our businesses."

—Luther Coggin
President and CEO
Coggin-O'Steen Investment Corporation

Let's Get Results, Not Excuses!—right on target! I became aware of the profound truth of this assertion when, as CEO of Porsche AG, I became involved in automobile racing. The fiercely competitive climate that has characterized automobile racing and other sports for some time occurs increasingly in all of our businesses. They key to success in these circumstances lies in a 'culture'—a mutually supportive team in which focus is on results, and excuses have no role!"

—Peter Schutz
CEO, retired
Porsche AG

"This dynamic approach to management is right on course! Excuses have always been accepted by my managers, and I have learned that if our new culture is such that we don't tolerate excuses anymore, the employees are less likely to make them. Logically speaking, there is nothing left to expect but results. Thanks for this common sense concept!"

—Chuck Weeder
Chairman
Homes of Merit, Inc.

"A provocative thesis that challenges assumptions of a committed workforce and some excellent recommendations for improving employee productivity and accountability."

—Bill Williams
President and CEO
TEC—An International Organization of CEOs

"The secret to standing out in your industry and getting true results is to be special, different, and unique. The most effective way to do this is to get rid of excuses in your organization. I highly recommend this book to all managers for the purpose of eliminating excuses from their company."

—Rick Martinell
Executive VP of Operations
Chi-Chi's, Inc.

"My coach, Woody Hayes, used to say, 'You're better than think you are, and I don't want excuses!' After reading this book, corporate leaders will better understand that to excel, neither can they tolerate excuses in the workplace."

—Tom Sladany
All-Pro Punter
3-Time All-American

"The Leadership Development Center has taken our organization from an excuse-laden sales culture to one that is totally results-oriented. Now results aren't everything, they are the only thing."

—Scott Lilja
Director of Training and Development
FinishMaster, Inc.

"The authors have done a great job of assembling a number of practical approaches to a very common business dilemma, that of excuse-making. The book is informative, easy to read, and filled with good information."

—C.P. Steimnetz
CEO
All-American Termite and Pest Control

"In my industry excuses have always been a deterrent to success. The frustrations that they cause can be eliminated when the excuses disappear! Thanks for such a simple and direct approach."

—Philip Voluck
President and CEO
Nutri/Systems, Inc.

"This book hits the mark! Bleech and Mutchler are on target—when you rid your environment of excuse-making, it is easier to manage others and get the results that you expect. I recommend this book for anyone in a management position."

—Jon Loftis
President
ECI Cemetery Services, Inc.

"If you want results, excuses must go. This book demonstrates the truth of this principle in the corporate world just as it is true in the athletic arena."

—Archie Griffin
2-Time Heisman Trophy Winner
3-Time All-American

"Occasionally, a book comes along which serves as a prelude to a major paradigm shift. *Let's Get Results, Not excuses!* is such a book. It accurately diagnoses the contagious excuse-making epidemic afflicting America's businesses. More importantly, it prescribes the remedies needed by corporate leaders to cure their organization of the disease. A must read for every executive and manager!"

—James I. Scon
Publisher
Success Club Magazine

"This book is simple, yet powerful. Unbelievably easy reading for a book so profound! I am now clear how to fully implement the promise of TQM and transform my organization to get results."

—Latry Brown
President
Brown Distributing Company

"Bleech and Mutchler clearly point out how corporate American can regain the lead in quality service through leadership at all levels of the organization."

—Corey Coughlin, CEO
South Trust Bank of Jacksonville

"I was mortified to see just how often excuses are given, and worse, we accept them! This book provides sound measures to put an end to this destructive pattern."

—Mark Richardson
President
Tortura & Company

"This is the most exciting concept in management I have ever seen. The authors have done a remarkable job of taking a very difficult concept and simplifying it in such a way that it can be swiftly implemented. I know if I get rid of excuses in my company, my results will greatly improve."

—Barry Grahek, CEO
Shred All, Inc.

"What a remarkable approach! If everyone paid attention to this message, millions would be added to our corporate bottom lines."

—George Bennett
President
BBS, Inc.

"Like a stealth bomber, excuses have infiltrated my management techniques. A few minutes with this book convinced me that I, the CEO, was making an excuse to accept the excuses of my associates. No more!"

—Carlton H. Spence
Chairman, CEO
Industrial Cold Storage

"Finally someone has hit the nail on the head! All of the seminars, books, schools, and lectures won't cure accountability. As long as business owners and managers accept excuses, the strength of our businesses will keep declining. When accountability is expected, the levels of management should decrease because there will be a lot less 'buck-passing.' A great book, and not a day too soon."

—Roy Mohrman
President
Handling Systems Engineering, Inc.

"I never realized how excuses were related to so many of our other management problems. It now seems so simple: eliminate excuses and everything else takes care of itself. Thanks for the insight!"

—Shirley Barton
President
American Medical Review

"Let's Get Results, Not Excuses! brilliantly combines principles of business and psychology into a simple action plan to get things done right on time, the first time. It is must reading for anyone who manages human behavior, including their own, in the business world or anywhere else."

—Kenneth Sass
District Manager
Waddell & Reed Financial Services

"This book is long overdue! It has opened my eyes. And I believe it is destined to be the force that awakens a sleeping corporate America."

—David Pugh
Bell South Communications

"So often I have looked at corrective actions directed towards my people. Neither I nor our executive team ever saw the relationship between our organizational structure and our processes as they related to improving the acceptance of responsibility by our people. This is truly one of the most exciting concepts I have ever read."

—Mike Johnson
OmniAmerica

"We have put up with mediocrity in this country for too long. We must get back on track. Excuses in the workplace create lack of focus and much shirking of responsibility. People need to be held accountable. This book is a strong, positive answer to many long-standing organizational problems."

—Marilyn Plank
Vice-President,
SYLVAN LEARNING CENTERS
of West Michigan

"Customers will always decide when they have had one excuse too many. The authors have pointed out how leadership can provide the guidance necessary to minimize those excuses, get the business, and provide superior customer service."

—Patrick C Kelly
Chairman, CEO
PSS

Dedication

To all leaders in corporate
America—past, present, and
future—committed to the cause
of becoming and remaining
number one in the marketplace.

About the Authors

James M. Bleech

James is Chairman of the Board of the Leadership Development Center. He is a former CPA and is presently a certified Professional Consultant to Management. In his 25 years of private industry experience he has had positions including Chief Operating Officer of a large multi-national construction firm and CEO of a high-profile business in the service sector. Since 1989, Jim has been consulting with leaders in numerous companies ranging from the small entrepreneur to the Fortune 500 senior executive. He is a highly sought-after public speaker and seminar leader. His expertise has been primarily in the areas of sales and marketing growth and personal leadership skills development for CEOs.

Dr. David G. Mutchler

David is the President and CEO of Leadership Development Center, a firm that provides leadership services to a wide range of businesses. He is a Certified Consultant to management and a member of the National Bureau of Professional Management Consultants. For several years he was a secondary and college level educator, during which time he coached many football teams to championship caliber. For the past several years, David has worked as a business trainer and consultant both nationally and internationally. He is doctorally trained in psychology and holds graduate degrees in philosophy and social work. His expertise has been primarily in the areas of corporate communication, and personal and organizational leadership development.

Table of Contents

Acknowledgments

It would be impossible to single out all the people who contributed so generously to this project with their comments, suggestions, and ideas. We owe a deep deity of gratitude to all, and a special thanks in that regard to our business manager, Carol Waite.

Many readers will know of an international organization called the Executive Committee, which is dedicated to the accelerated development of CECOs. Jim, as chairman of one of the 400 TEC groups, has met many unique resource speakers who have contributed greatly to our thinking. While something has been gained from each, two individuals in particular have added to the breadth of our knowledge. Peter Schutz, former CEO of Porsche AG, not only gave us insight, but also the courage to tackle the project. Peter introduced the concept of *organization, process, and people*, which has become a central part of our book. Del Poling, independent consultant extraordinaire, first introduced us to the importance of recognizing excuses, as well as how dangerous they can become to a company. We owe the concept of *four-year-old behavior* to him.

Without doubt, our biggest source of material has been the clients we've served over the years who have talked openly about their problems and concerns. It was the many late-hour discussions and painful board meeting with them that furnished our first glimmer of awareness that we were conceiving a very different approach to effective management. In effect, our clients have been our laboratory for the gradual testing and development of excuse-free behavior for use in corporate America.

We are grateful for the wisdom of Stephen Covey and W. Edwards Deeming. Their thinking helped form the cornerstone for many of our ideas. Also, as season ticket holders we appreciate the example set by Don Shula of the Miami Dolphins for creating an extraordinary organization with extraordinary processes—a model that we have built much of the book around.

A special thanks to our editor, Gwyn Bersie, whose tireless effort helped keep us focused and on course. Her insight, guidance, and editorial talents are dearly appreciated.

Finally, to our wives, many thanks. They have generously worn several hats throughout this project: proofreaders, sounding boards, single parents when necessary, and sources of love, strength, and support. Without them, this book would never have happened.

Preface

As I look back to the original printing of *Let's Get Results, Not Excuses*, I remember how proud I was to see my first book in the bookstores. However, nothing makes me as proud as the realization of a business book, and a growing number of very large companies continue to use this book as an important component of their management and leadership training programs.

When the decision was made to go through yet another reprint, our publisher asked what change we wanted to make to the content. Upon reviewing the text, I found I wanted to change everything and nothing.

Since the original publication, I had the opportunity to work with hundreds of companies who are interested in getting rid of the disease of excuse-making.

As I worked with these organizations, I developed a missionary zeal of helping people accept responsibility and quit making excuses. In the process, I have become totally immersed in our message.

As is true in any important endeavor, however, it is not long before you realize you are just scratching the surface. That's what I wanted to change in this edition of the book. I wanted to add all of the other things I have learned. I wanted to better address the larger issue of organizational culture and values alignment. I wanted to talk more about strategies and visions and how to ensure that they are congruent with the culture that exists in an organization. And most important, I wanted to address the concept of aligning personal and organizational values. All of these issues are critically important to the ultimate elimination of excuses.

However, as I began to outline these changes, I realized they are complex issues that would take hundreds of additional pages and could easily obscure the clear, simple, and concise message of the original book. Therefore, I chose not to dilute our message, but to let it stand in the format that has made this book so successful over the past six years. Perhaps at a later date, I will address those other issues. For now, let's keep it simple: Let's Get Results, Not Excuses!

James M. Bleech
Leadership Development Center
645 Mayport Road, Suite 6
Atlantic Beach, Fl 32233
August, 2002

Notes and Quotes

Ninety-nine percent of the failures come from people who have the habit of making excuses.

George Washington Carver

PART I:
The Nature
of the Problem

The Relationship Between
Results and Excuses

CHAPTER 1

A Wolf in Sheep's Clothing

Let's Start with a Modified
Fable That Has Business
Relevance...

A certain wolf could not get to the sheep because of the watchfulness of the shepherd and his dogs. But one day he found a sheepskin that, after flaying, had been cast aside and forgotten.

The next day, the wolf disguised himself by throwing the skin over his body, and strolled in the pasture among the sheep. Before long a little lamb was following him about and was quickly led away and eaten. This continued over time, unbeknownst to the shepherd, so that gradually the flock was greatly reduced in number, and the shepherd's profits were reduced to near zero.

The moral of the story:

Beware of dangerous things that become familiar, and thus appear harmless!

Excuses are wolves in sheep's clothing!

From a Supervisory Point of View, Can You Relate with Any of the Following?

Warren is the director of human resources at a company that employs 134 people. Last month he asked his assistant, Jim, to research three alternative benefit plans in preparation for changing vendors at the beginning of the fiscal year. Warren had advised Jim that the research was due today.

Warren: "Are you finished researching the benefit plans?"

Jim: "I've made some progress on it, but I've been extremely busy putting the finishing touches on another project." (the *busyness* excuse)

Warren: "You know how important this matter is to the company. When do you think it will be completed?"

Jim: "I should have it done in another week or two."

Fred is a sales representative for a mid-sized optical firm. As part of a plan to generate new accounts, he was instructed by his sales manager to call on three new optometrists per week in addition to servicing his existing accounts. At week's end, Fred's sales manager asked for the names, addresses, and phone numbers of the contact person for each of the new businesses.

Sales Manager: "What new accounts did you call on this week, Fred?"

Fred: "I was only able to contact one. I'll do the other two later." (**The** *procrastination* **excuse**)

Sales Manager: "Didn't I make it clear that you are to call onthree new accounts every week?"

Fred: "Yes, you made that clear."

Sales Manager: "Is there some reason you only called on one new account rather than three?"

Fred: "Yes I spent extra time with several of our currentcustomers getting additional orders. Look, here's the business I wrote this week, twice as much as I did the week before!"

Sales Manager: "I see that. Good job! But let's not forget to keep calling on new accounts."

Fred: "I won't forget."

Vince is the CEO of a $200 million paint company. He depends on his top four managers to furnish key indicators for the business every Monday morning in the executive planning session. This particular Monday, one of the managers, Steve, is unprepared.

Vince: "Okay, let's deal with the financials."

Steve: "The bank didn't get them back to us yet, so it was impossible for me to have them ready for the meeting." (the *projection of blame* excuse)

Vince: (somewhat upset) "But we depend on the financial reports to plan our entire month."
Steve: "I know, but it was out of my control." (the *denial of responsibility* excuse)

Vince: "Now what do we do?"

Steve: "Let's hope we get them today."

We've all been there, have we not? One excuse or another, some seemingly more legitimate than others, interferes with getting the results that we want. Here, Warren's plans are held up, causing delays in implementing a new benefit program; the optical company lost potential business because Fred didn't make inroads into the designated number of new accounts; and Vince and the other executives were slowed down in their efforts to plan the business month, costing them real dollars as a result.

The Point

Excuses are familiar. Very familiar. They happen all around us many, many times every day. They happen so often that they begin to appear harmless, which is one of the reasons they're so dangerous. But they aren't harmless. Just as the wolf was a threat to the sheep, excuses are a threat to our companies in ways that are difficult to detect and that we usually don't see coming beforehand.

Excuses Indicate Other Problems

While excuses may appear harmless because they are so familiar, they are *anything but* harmless. Excuses are inseparably linked to more serious organizational problems that silently undermine our corporations on a daily basis. That makes excuses *gigantic* problems because wherever there is an excuse, there—lurking in the shadows—is the destructive context necessary for that excuse to exist.

For Example

· "They weren't interested in what I had to say when they made this decision, so this shouldn't be my responsibility now." (the context:**denial of responsibility**)

· "We're late with the report because purchasing was late getting it to us." (the context: **projection of blame**)

· "I've been very busy these past few weeks; I'll get to it as soon as possible." (the context: **procrastination**)

· "I lost the account because the competition undercut our prices," rather than "I lost the account because I haven't been servicing it well." (the context: **self-deceit, denial of responsibility, projection of blame**)

· "I was never trained adequately to do this job." (the context: **incompetence, denial of responsibility**)

· "We've never done it that way before," or "That's not the way we do things around here." (The context: **lack of stretching, taking risks, and being creative**)

· "It's not my fault that the order was messed up. I still deserve my bonus." (the context: **attitude of entitlement**)

• "We're never going to catch up to the competition. Everybody's so far ahead of us in so many ways." (The context: **pessimism**)

These insidious behaviors—and more—are the *real* poisons in our companies today. Together, they make up the culture in which excuse-making can exit. Most people would agree that any organization that could purge itself of denial of responsibility, projection of blame, procrastination, and so on would soon stand head and shoulders above the competition. Yet it is new and unusual to think that the way to achieve this is by getting rid of excuse-making. Instead, the norm has been to tolerate or ignore excuses.

We Are Going to Challenge This Point of View

The basic premise of this book is that *in the corporate setting, excuse making is more than just an annoyance.* **It is a huge problem. In fact, it may be the biggest single problem that exists in corporate America. Why? Because excuses always indicate the presence of other conditions—denial of responsibility, projection of blame, procrastination, etc.—that sooner or later bring an organization to its knees. The good news is that when excuse-making is eliminated from the corporate scene, all of these other destructive behaviors go away, and results follow naturally.**

What Comes Next?

In the remaining chapters of Part I we will lay the foundation necessary to make sense of this revolutionary perspective. We will look at what excuses are, why they happen, and what makes them generally so dangerous. In Part II we will explore the scope of the problem of excuses in our corporations by examining how they influence a company's culture, leadership, planning processes, and teamwork, as well as how they infect bureaucracies overall. In Part III we will guide you step by step through the process of diagnosing the excuse-making virus in your company and of applying the effective treatment(s) for your specific situation.

A Final Thought

A problem well defined is a problem half-solved, that is, recognition of the real problem is half the battle. The fact is that people are more accustomed to thinking of excuses as a *minor problem* in our companies *rather* than as *the major problem*. Individuals *who* are making this shift in thinking—persons like you from companies of all sizes—are finding remarkable results, which shouldn't be surprising. The relationship between excuse-making and results is like the relationship between night and day—they is opposites, and therefore they are mutually exclusive.

Consequently, when you get rid of excuses, results follow naturally. It can't be any other way. Those companies, therefore, that make the elimination of excuses their number one priority stand to become the clear winners in the increasingly competitive race to succeed.

CHAPTER 2

Reason or Excuse? It's a Tough Call

A question we often hear from managers when they first embrace the notion of eliminating excuses from the workplace is, "How will we know whether a person is giving us a legitimate reason or if he is just making a lame excuse?" This question assumes that to get rid of excuses you must be able to *differentiate* a reason from an excuse. We will challenge this assumption in the next chapter, but for now let's examine the question, "What is the difference between a reason and an excuse?"

A Brief Quiz

Suppose you manage the following individuals. Given the situations listed below, would you conclude that the explanation each person gives is a **reason**, an **excuse**, or is **not clear** (that is, there's not enough information to decide)?

- Mark is 45 minute, late for work. You ask him where he's been, and he responds that he was held up in traffic due to an auto accident.

    Reason   **Excuse**   **Not Clear**

- David missed an important meeting today. His wife called to say that he has the flu and won't be coming into work.

    Reason   **Excuse**   **Not Clear**

- Larry was to have, a project completed by 10:00. It is not finished yet at 4:30, and he reports that it was held up because data processing was late getting some of the required information to him.

    Reason   **Excuse**   **Not Clear**

- Cheryl informs you that her work team is behind schedule due to the sudden and unexpected resignation of two of its four members.

    Reason   **Excuse**   **Not Clear**

It's Really a Matter of Perception and Personal Judgment

If you answered these four questions like most people, you probably chose "not clear" in each case. The reality is that people *usually* don't have sufficient information to *determine* the difference between an excuse and a reason, just as you experienced in the preceding exercise. This is a real problem because it allows for the vast majority of excuses to pass as reasons and reasons—if they are even marginally believable—are typically accepted as true.

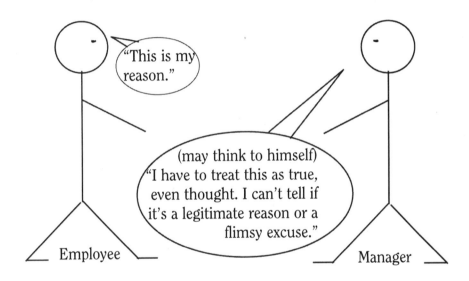

Figure 1

Again, it is nearly impossible to distinguish an excuse from a reason, regardless of whether the excuse is valid or invalid, good or bad, right or wrong. The two look and sound so much alike that it is far easier—and in most situations, more respectful—simply to accept an explanation as "reasonable" at face value without questioning it. This is true even if a little voice inside may be saying "this person is really trying to *pull the wool over my eyes*"—***like the wolf in sheep's clothing.***

The Problem Magnified

This blurring of the boundaries between reasons and excuses is precisely what happens in our companies, only on a much larger scale. In the context of the work place, the confusion between the two multiplies exponentially. As the number of employees, managers, departments, divisions, processes, systems, and functions increase, so does the opportunity for excuse-making. Subsequently, excuses run rampant in our companies, causing extensive damage to the bottom lines. Not overnight, of course, because the damage is difficult to detect from day to day, just as it is difficult to see cancer grow from one day to the next. But measured in months and years, the damage progresses just as surely as cancer grows; and as with cancer, so with excuses—if the growth of the problem isn't checked, it will, over time, virtually destroy the body on which it feeds.

The Dilemma

It would appear, then, that we are faced with a choice between two alternatives, both of which are equally unworkable. On the one hand, excuses must go, since they are quietly yet methodically eroding away the profits in our corporations. On the other hand, excuses are so difficult to discern from legitimate reasons that it looks like nothing can really be done to work on the problem. It is in this state of confusion that excuse-making has gone unchecked, costing organizations megadollars day after day, month after month, and year after year.

So What is a Company to Do?

We need no longer remain hopelessly trapped by the parameters of our own thinking. Fortunately, we now can eliminate excuses in our companies, and when we do, results follow. But that requires a total redefinition of the problem, an approach from an entirely different perspective, the consequence of which is that it allows us to work on the elimination of excuse-making in a powerfully new way.

Notes and Quotes

An excuse is worse and more terrible than a lie; for an excuse is a lie guarded.

Pope

CHAPTER 3

An Excuse Is an Excuse Is an Excuse...

It is no secret that American business has fallen from first place in terms of its status in the global market place. In some ways we have made a remarkable turnaround in recent years, and much credit is due in this regard. But something is still missing, and that something is the central theme of this book, namely, **that the way to regain our position as number one is to make the elimination of excuses from the workplace our number one priority.**

Why Hasn't This Happened Before Now?

Actually, there are several explanations as to why the elimination of excuses from the workplace has been a low priority, if it has been a priority at all:

1. For the most part, corporate America *hasn't yet admitted* that excuses are in fact a large problem. Excuse-making has been accepted as a behavior that is natural to life, like eating, breathing, and sleeping. There has been no reason to try to fix something that we haven't perceived as broken.

2. In those instances where excuses have been recognized as a problem in our organizations, many have seen them only as *little* problems—nuisances, annoyances, irritations—clearly not something to give a whole lot of time and attention

3. For those who have admitted that excuse-making is a significant problem in their companies, the *tools required to eliminate excuses haven't been available.* It has been difficult, therefore, to do much about the problem, even for those who have been so motivated. Some have probably, tried, failed, and—understandably—given up.

4. Typically, when there are problems that humans can't resolve, we tend to develop perceptual blinders and act as if the problems aren't really there. We're like ostriches with our heads in the sand it's more tolerable if we deny the problem all together. For those few, then, who have tried to get rid of the problem of excuses but haven't had the necessary tools to do so, the problem would naturally *be minimized over time and eventually be ignored.*

5. Last, some few individuals have probably realized that the problem of excuses is, in fact, huge. They may even believe that it can be corrected, but think of it as such a monumental task that they *don't try* to do anything about it. The magnitude of the change effort seems too overwhelming.

Since These Approaches Haven't Worked, What Is the Answer?

First, we must *admit* that excuses are a problem in our companies. When a problem isn't recognized it can't be defined, and when it isn't defined it can't be corrected. Again, a problem well-defined is a problem half-solved.

Second, we must recognize that excuses are not just a problem, they are a serious problem in the workplace. So *serious*, in fact, that if left untreated, they are life threatening to any organization In the fast-changing business climate in which we live today, those companies that cannot adjust quickly to the demands of the marketplace are soon left behind. It is impossible to stay ahead of, or even keep abreast with, the competitive corporate race if excuses are allowed to be part of a company's culture in any way, shape, or form. Now more than ever before, *if you're not working to stay one step ahead, you're already falling behind.*

Third, *we cannot continue to use the lack of effective tools as an excuse to tolerate excuses in our companies, in the present.*

There are excellent tools available now, the details of which are spelled out in Part III of this book. The problem in the past is that we've viewed the whole problem of excuses—if we've viewed excuse-making as a problem at all—as one of trying to differentiate excuses from reasons **in individuals**, and this is a difficult task to accomplish. To discern one from the other requires either being confrontive with people by challenging their reasons, or by playing detective behind people's backs to see if they're telling the truth. Few people want to do either, so again, it's easier to give in and accept excuse-making as a fact of life.

Fourth, *we need no longer minimize and ignore* the problem of excuses in our organizations for lack of knowing what to do about it. Ridding our companies of excuses is now largely achievable. To minimize or ignore the reality of the problem from this point forth would be an excuse of the highest order.

Fifth, and in line with the above, *we must stop thinking that the problem of excuses is so overwhelming that it isn't even worth trying to solve.* The problem only

19

seems overwhelming because we haven't before understood it. The bubonic plague and polio, as with so many diseases throughout history, seemed overwhelming until we fully understood them. Now both are easily managed. So it is with eliminating excuses from the workplace. Now that the problem is fully understood, it is not of such magnitude that we can't tackle it. In fact, solving the problem is not nearly as complex as it may seem at first glance.

What Are These New Tools?

That's really what the rest of this book is all about. Briefly, and by way of introduction, _the secret to eliminating excuses from the workplace is to act from foresight rather than hindsight. It is to **stop** working on whether or not this or that excuse is valid, and to **start** working on the reasons why people make excuses at all. This is achieved by getting rid of the **conditions under which** people make excuses._

For Example

Suppose Lori is to have a report to Brad by 3:00 on Friday afternoon. Suppose further that when the report is due, Lori informs Brad that she had several interruptions that kept her from meeting the deadline. The question now should not be "Is this a legitimate excuse?" To ask that question is to work on the wrong end of the problem, namely, _on the validity or invalidity of an excuse **given by an individual**, after the fact._

Instead, questions need to be asked _before the fact_. "How important is it to have the report completed on time?" "What night come up that would interfere with meeting the deadline?" "What can be done to handle these possibilities so the deadline can still be met?" "What are the consequences of not finishing the report on time? _"This approach eliminates excuses by **preventing** them be forehand rather than judging them afterward"._

In Addition...

It doesn't work if you:

• **pretend that people's excuses are good reasons, which is the traditional approach. To do so is to deny the reality of the situation.**

• **confront people by telling them that you think their reason is really an excuse, since people fear conflict.**

• **play detective and work behind the scenes to determine whether or not the person is telling you the truth. This presumes lack of trust   in people's integrity.**

The Winning Formula

Clearly, we must take a strong stand that "no excuses are allowed." But this does **not** mean that leaders and managers can be dictators and mandate that people can't give excuses in their organizations. Since excuses are self-protective, this would soon cause a complete breakdown of communication, as people would stop talking all together when faced with the need to protect themselves from blame, criticism, or failure.

To the contrary, "no excuses allowed" means that those in charge must have foresight to prepare the structures and processes sufficiently *beforehand* so that excuses never have to be made. For example, if it had been set up that Lori had a 3:00 deadline, agreed to that deadline, understood that it was top priority, had backup to plans to ensure its completion, and consented to the consequences if not completed on schedule, *why would there be any need for a reason or an excuse?*

Let's say it differently. Suppose that the contingencies were not given the proper attention ahead of time to prevent any chance for excuses. If Lori misses the deadline and justifies her actions by saying that there were several important interruptions, *does it really matter whether her explanation is valid or not?* **Who cares?** What matters is that the results were ***not*** achieved! The question is not whether she has a legitimate explanation for not completing the task, but rather, did she understand the importance of the deadline, were backup plans spelled out to ensure its completion, and did she understand the consequences of not getting it done on the schedule agreed?

The point is, the reason the job didn't get done, the reason the desired results were not achieved, was *because of the inadequacy of the setup*. This principle of "setup," what we will later call "organization" and "processes," must become of paramount concern.

Therefore

From this point forth, the word "excuse" will be used whenever the purpose of someone's explanation is to justify himself. In the end, *it doesn't matter whether his explanation is valid or invalid, legitimate or illegitimate right or wrong, true or false, reason or excuse.* **All that matters is results,** *and that happens by making sure the setup—that is, the organization and the processes—is correct in advance mutual agreements, prioritization, backup plans, consequences for not living to the agreements, and so on. When the setup is correct, the systems are then in place to significantly reduce the incidence of excuses in our corporations, and results follow.*

And Last

Since excuse-making is a silent killer in our organizations, and since it is a slow-creeping deadly disease, it clearly must be eliminated. In order to accomplish this, it is helpful to understand the source of the disease, and how excuse-making can be fatal to a company. The remainder of Part I addresses these issues.

Notes and Quotes

We are all manufacturers—making good, making trouble, or making excuses.

A .V. Adolt

CHAPTER 4

The Source of the Disease

Time out for a brief lesson in pain and how human beings deal with painful situations.

Excuses Can Help a Person Feel Better

Nobody likes to hurt. This is true physically, mentally, and emotionally. We human beings have many wonderful mechanisms built into our system to defend ourselves against feeling pain. The state of shock after a person is injured in an accident is a classic example. While in shock, one may not feel any pain for several hours while the body rallies its defenses to handle the trauma that it has just experienced.

The same principle is true of us as psychological beings. Experiments have been conducted where a special pair of glasses is used to invert a person's field of vision so that everything is seen as upside down. In a relatively short period of time, amazingly, a person wearing these same glasses will begin to see everything right side up! What's more, when the lenses are removed the world appears once again temporarily upside down. Soon, however, the person will begin to see the world right side up.

The point is that the human mind is a miraculously powerful thing. It does whatever it can to insure our survival in this world. Since pain in a human being

of any kind always signals danger, it is the job of the various systems of the mind and body to put a stop to the feeling of danger by eliminating the source of the pain. Psychologically speaking, this means that whenever possible the mind will do whatever it can to keep from hurting. One of the ways our minds have figured out how to do this is to—you guessed it—*make excuses*.

How It Happens: Example #1

Let's take a closer look. Mark, a well-mannered new salesperson on the job, is not meeting quotas. For five consecutive months he has fallen short. His sales manager has informed him that in order to meet his required level of sales, he must make a minimum of five cold calls every day. Mark hates cold calls, so he doesn't make them. But listen to what he telles his wife when she complains that he's not earning enough money to support the family. "I can't help it that my sales are down. I just don't have a good territory!" This is an excuse on Mark's part. Why did he make an excuse rather than tell his wife the real reason that his sales are insufficient? Because it kept him *at that moment* from hurting. Mark was avoiding two potential sources of pain—one that might come from his wife's response, the other from what he would feel if admitted the real reason to himself.

How It Happens: Example #2

Sally is, in general, a talented and valuable member of an office staff. Her office manager has asked her to give a joint presentation on some newly acquired word processing capabilities to the engineering department. Sally agrees to co-present with her supervisor, though she is petrified of having to speak in front of a group.

On the morning that the presentation is planned, Sally calls her manager to report that she was very ill in the night, and that she will not be able to help with the presentation. The fact is that she didn't sleep well because she was so concerned about having to stand up in front of the engineers. But if she told her manager the truth, it would hurt. Instead, she made an excuse in order to protect herself from the pain.

Notice one additional dimension to Sally's interaction with her supervisor: *The excuse she gave is one that her boss will accept.* The fact that an excuse is acceptable in the eyes of the person to whom one is making it adds tremendous power to the potential for excuse-making. We will visit this notion again later.

Our Potential for Making Excuses Is Inborn

We don't need to be taught to make excuses. As part of the self-protective nature of the brain, we are born with the raw materials necessary to make spontaneous, appropriate, ingenious, and instantaneous excuses. It has nothing to do with having evil thoughts or being a bad person. Put an individual in an experience where the truth about himself might hurt, and there you have an excuse in the making.

We Also Learn to Make Excuses

To say that we don't need to be taught to make excuses is not to imply that we aren't also taught. Indeed, we begin to learn which excuses to make, and when to make them, at a very early age. Two-year-old Jimmy sees his four-year-old brother Scott getting away with not eating the vegetables he doesn't like with the excuse, "I'm full, Mommy." Thus it is that Jimmy learns quickly that excuse-making is allowed. So he tries it out for himself. "And Jimmy, why aren't you eating your vegetables?" "Because I'm full, too, Mommy!"

It doesn't take long for our young brains, already predisposed to make excuses whenever possible in order to sidestep pain, to learn exactly when and how to do it. Excuse-making is the way the young child learns to maneuver in his or her world. We need only get away with making an excuse one time for the process to be reinforced and for the excuse-making mindset to be put into motion. In the words of Sven Wahlroos, in his book *Excuses: How to Spot Them, Deal with Them, and Stop Using Them,* "If children are allowed to get away with using excuses, some of which may originally have been deliberate, the excuses will become automatic reflexes by the time they reach adulthood." (1981, p. 6).

What he doesn't say is that in the average child's life, he or she is allowed to get away with excuses on many, many occasions. Dad sometimes makes excuses to Mom, Mom sometimes makes excuses to Dad, parents on occasion make excuses to their children, children learn to make excuses to their parents. The patterns become well rehearsed at an early age. This is why we may refer to excuse-making occasionally as **four-year-old behavior**. Because by that age we have all been well-prepared to function in the world—a world where excuses are not only allowed, but are also unknowingly encouraged and reinforced.

Excuses and Not-Okness

This is an aside, but we think an important one. A whole chapter, perhaps an entire book, could be given to this subject, but a quick overview is all we have space for here.

Many a child is raised hearing from time to time that he or she is worthless, no good, inferior, "in the way," to be seen and not heard, a "bad" boy or a "bad" girl. The conclusion many children reach as a result is that they are Not OK persons. Suppose that a child's mother and father are under extreme financial stress. In a moment of intense frustration Dad shouts at Mom, "I wish the kids had never been born—they cost too damn much money!" What does a small child conclude in this situation, especially if this statement—powerful because it was made in an emotional moment—is never corrected? Sometimes what's not said speaks louder than what is said.

Nor does the problem stop in the home. The same phenomenon carries forward to school and society. For example, schools typically view failure by children as unacceptable rather than as a valuable learning experience. Consequently, when a child fails at something, he or she is usually disciplined rather than encouraged. Far too often in this situation children conclude that they are Not OK, and much damage is done to their young psyches.

When a child concludes that he or she may be Not OK, it hurts a lot! It hurts so much that it may lead the child to grow up making excuses whenever telling the truth could bring on the feeling that, deep down, he or she may be Not OK. An excuse helps one in that moment to feel OK.

Excuse-Making as Normal vs. Abnormal Behavior

This is where the line between rationalization and excuse-making gets a little fuzzy. When we feel Not OK about ourselves at some deep level, weak egos—and therefore an abundance of rationalizations—set in. The deeper the pain, the more pronounced is the rationalization. In its extreme forms, one doesn't have to be a trained psychologist to spot this kind of behavior.

A man had been bragging incessantly about his boat to an acquaintance. Tiring of the story, his acquaintance asked the man if he could see the boat. The man replied that he would love to give him a ride in his own personal 150-foot luxury yacht. The problem was, it was _so_ big that it had to be anchored several miles off shore, too far out to be seen from land. It seems that the motor on his smaller boat that he used to get to it was broken down, so he was sorry, but the offer would just have to wait until another time.

Most people would not have difficulty recognizing this story as an untruth. But it is more than just a lie. It is a blatant rationalization used to cover the fact that the man didn't have a boat of any sort, although reporting that he did helped him feel more OK at the time.

This example is purposely used to illustrate that when we mention excuse-making in this book, we are not referring, as with this man, to some pathological condition whose source is a deep-seated feeling of Not-OKness. Most people feel OK enough about themselves that they don't have to rely on extreme rationalizations or outright lies to keep from hurting emotionally.

Normal People Don't Like to Hurt Either

Nevertheless, it is important to keep in mind that "normal" people, the vast majority who feel mostly OK themselves, don't like emotional discomfort, either. But the rationalizations of normal people are qualitatively different from those of the man and his luxury boat. They are much less obvious, and far more invisible, pervasive, and commonplace. They form a language all their own—the *language of excuse-making*. It is a language that, by and large, is an acceptable language in our culture. Its power, and its danger, lies in its invisibility and subtlety. It is a language we all learn at a very young and formative age. It is a language that expresses a chronic disease of the times—the disease of excusitis. And it must be eliminated in the workplace if we are going to fix corporate America.

And Last

Thus it is that we become skilled at making excuses early in our lives. Sadly, that same skill continues to develop throughout life because it continues to find fertile soil in which to grow and multiply. One of the places where the soil is most fertile for its expression is in the corporations of this country. Let's press on and look more closely at what this means.

CHAPTER 5

Excuses Indicate Other Problems

When it comes to excuses, the world is an interesting place. It is a bit of a paradox. A high premium is placed on responsibility, at least in terms of lessons taught. Parents give us important messages about responsibility. "Pick up after yourself, Jane." Teachers tell us it is important to take responsibility for ourselves. "Make sure your homework assignment is completed, students." Boy Scout and Girl Scout troop leaders teach us to be responsible individuals. "Do a good turn daily." Priests, pastors, nuns, church schools—more lessons about how important it is to be a responsible person.

But in practice, the world doesn't always work that way. Not only are excuses allowed (remember Sally and her excuse about being ill and therefore not able to present to a group of engineers), they also are encouraged and reinforced. That they are allowed is somewhat easily understood. Personal illness is an excellent case in point. Rarely is sickness questioned so long as it is not overdone. But what of the fact that many companies actually have acknowledged "sick days" as part of their benefits package? Since people aren't paid extra if they don't take them, are we thereby encouraging people to take sick days without really being sick? Are we making it easier for people to make excuses?

A Common Situation

Let's take a closer look at the suggestion that the workplace may actually encourage and reinforce excuses.

Richard is a sharp individual. He began his career in middle management at a sizeable corporation on the East Coast within weeks after he graduated from an Ivy League business school. His superiors recognized early on that Richard had great potential for moving up the management ranks in the business world. He showed considerably more initiative in solving problems than those who had preceded him. He was the envy of others in middle management with whom he worked. After 18 months on the job, he was promoted. Nine months later, a second promotion. After four years, Richard found himself already in an upper management position. While

34

Richard had numerous skills and talents in the corporate environment including being a natural leader and communicator, his real forte had always been, and still is, his ability to identify and solve problems.

Today Richard is 53 years old. He is the CEO of another large company. But there are problems. He has been divorced twice, unable to sustain his marital relationships in large part because of the long hours he puts in at work. His health is failing under the weight of the never-ending stress of his job. Now, as always in the past, he is heavily burdened by the problems that confront him daily in his business. He voices his concern in terms of how much easier things would be if the managers who report directly to him would take more responsibility in solving some of the problems that he is left with. "They just don't seem to take any responsibility around here," is a comment he has been heard to say on more than one occasion.

Richard's story is not an uncommon one. He is but one of thousands of executives who are good people, strong leaders, respected individuals, hard workers, but who experience trouble brewing at some level that is difficult for them to put their finger on. It is the source of considerable fustration. In addition, they know it is costing their companies a great deal of money.

What Richard and the countless numbers of executives like him don't know is that he may be unwittingly encouraging and reinforcing the very cause of his own problem. Think about it a minute. Richard fought his way to the top through his ability to solve problems. How is he going to assure himself and others that he has what it takes to *stay* at the top? Inside, he feels that he must continue to perform well at the same skills that got him there. **He must continue to solve problems.**

It is impossible to solve problems unless there are problems to be solved. To say it bluntly, Richard must have problems in order to function.

The Return to Four-Year-Old Rules.

When the unspoken corporate ethos, or culture, is that Richard must have problems to solve in order to function well in his position, two things will happen. First, though unaware of the fact that he is doing so, Richard will surround himself with—to one degree or another—*dependent* people who know quite well how to play by the rules. Second, these same people will arrange for Richard to receive more than his share of problems. Why? To please their boss. How? *All they have to do is play by the same rules that they learned as four-year-olds*. Make excuses—it works every time. I couldn't do it because it was this department's fault. This department couldn't do it because it was that department's fault. I blame you. You blame someone else. They blame yet someone else. And so on, sometimes without end.

The consequence: problems do not get solved, matters do not get handled, desired results are not achieved. No one person in the corporate structure can be held responsible because there are so many interdependent parts. One by one, the problems get passed up to Richard's desk. By the time the problem gets to Richard, it is surrounded by so many excuses that he has a difficult time understanding what the real problem is. The real problem may be that X didn't get done. But the excuses relate to it being Y department's fault. So Richard may concentrate on Y and miss the heart of the real problem.

Thus it is that Richard gets more than his share of problems. It is sometimes overwhelming. He tries to figure it out. He thinks he sees the problem, and he even tries to fix it. "They just don't make managers like they used to." Fire this one. Train that one. Hire yet another.

Ultimately, none of his solutions work. Why? Because he has only been able to see pieces of the problem rather than the bigger picture. What is happening in that bigger picture? Is it Richard's doing? Yes and no. Is it his managers' fault? Yes and no. Is it the people downline for their unwillingness to take responsibility? Yes and no. It is all of the above, and more. It's the mixture of many elements coming together in such a way that the results are less than desirable. It is excuse-making run rampant, and corporations surviving, even if barely, in spite of themselves.

Excuses Point to Other Problems

There are two fundamental reasons why we set forth the hypothesis that excuse-making is so critically important as a core issue in corporate America. We will discuss the first of these reasons here, the second later.

Wherever excuses exist in the workplace, there we will find in existence several other related—and usually invisible—destructive forces in operation, forces that interfere directly with achieving desired results. Excuses are like the tip of an iceberg: fairly big in and of itself, but only a small chunk compared to the rest that lies beneath the surface. For all that we see, there is much more that we don't see.

Those who navigate in waters where icebergs exist are well aware that the danger to their ship is the part of the iceberg that lies beneath the water and out of sight, not the part that shows. This is exactly the way it is with excuses. It is the parts that don't show, the ones you don't readily see that you need to be concerned about the most.

Figure 2

Let's take a look at some of these destructive forces that form the body of the iceberg beneath the surface of excuses.

Victimization

Where there are excuses, there—if we poke around a bit—we will invariably find hiding what is known as a "victimization mindset."

Definition

Vic-tim-i-za-tion, n. The state of being victimized; the attitude that one is a victim of influences *outside of one's control,* thus robbing an individual of the personal power to change his or her set of undesirable circumstances.

An Example from the Olympics

Our society is a veritable hotbed of the victimization mentality. We were reminded of that again by the 1994 Winter Olympic Games. The United States' own Nancy Kerrigan was edged out for the gold medal by Aksana Baiul of the Ukraine by the narrowest of split decisions. Immediately afterward, where was the American press? Noisily interviewing each other trying to convince themselves of Kerrigan's victimization. After all, Ms. Kerrigan did two combination jumps, including a difficult triple-toe, tripie-toe loop. Baiul did only one combination, a double-double. Some Kerrigan supporters pointed out that the Ukrainian judge was the father of Baiul's ex-coach. Get it? *Some judge victimized Nancy because he was partial to her opponent!*

And thus we showed the world our way of thinking: **It must be someone else's fault.**

Victimization and the Legal System

Another example of the victimization mindset in our society can be found in our legal system. One could debate whether the system encourages and supports people to think as victims, or whether it is simply responding to the way people think on their own. Probably some of both is true. Either way, the victimization mentality certainly reaches deep into our system of jurisprudence. *It must be somebody (or something) else's fault.* Few would argue against the premise that we are the most lawsuit-happy nation in the world. For example, here is a man who, in a state of inebriation, crosses the center line in his vehicle and collides head-on with a car carrying a family of five. All five people in the other vehicle are killed. The inebriated driver experiences whiplash, and for several months thereafter, chronic neck pain. What happens? The drunken driver sues the bar and bartender for being responsible for his drunkenness, the collision, and the whiplash. What's even more interesting? He wins!

Procrastination

Where there are excuses, there—if we poke around a bit—we will invariably find hiding something known as procrastination. Typically, it can be found just beneath the surface, as with the iceberg. In other words, procrastination is rarely open and obvious. But when one finds it in operation, you can bet on the presence of excuses as well!

Definition

Pro-cras-ti-na-tion, n. *The act of putting off doing something until a future time; postponing or deferring action; delaying from day to day; waiting until tomorrow to do that which could be done today.*

Procrastination in Operation

George is the vice-president of operations at a $75 million-per-year midwestern trucking firm. In January he was asked by the senior vice-president to research the reasons why the drivers had been receiving an inordinate number of fines for carrying cargos that exceeded the normal weight limits. George agreed to take on the project, and promised to present the results at the next monthly meeting.

Subsequently, George was asked for the results of his study at the February executive committee meeting. He replied that he had been very busy, and that he would have it ready for the March meeting. His senior vice-president accepted George's answer, apparently unconcerned about what had now become commonplace (and therefore acceptable) at his company the *procrastination excuse*—one of the most commonly used excuses in business. At the March meeting the report still was not completed. George was asked why. "I'm sorry, sir. I was so busy that I assigned it to Frank, and Frank hasn't been able to get to it yet. He is working hard to complete another project. I'll do my best to have him submit it by next month."

Earlier we pointed out that **when you get excuses, you don't get results.** *George is a classic example of this principle in operation.*

Reactive Thinking

Where there are excuses, there—if we poke around a bit—we will find hiding what is known as "reactive thinking" and "reactive people" (as opposed to "proactive thinking" and "proactive people"). It probably won't be open and obvious, but if there are excuses, there will be reactive thinking. You can count on it.

Definition

Re-act-ive, adj. The state of responding to a stimulus; being affected by some influence, event, etc. **Re-act-ive. Thinking:** a way of conceptualizing experience such that one's behavior is seen as a function of conditions *outside of oneself* rather than as the result of one's own decisions and/or choices.

The Language of Reactive People

Stephen R. Covey in his bestseller, *The 7 Habits of Highly Effective People*, states:

The language of reactive people absolves them of responsibility. "That's me. That's just the way I am." *I am determined. There's nothing I can do about it.*

"He makes me so mad!" *I'm not responsible. My emotional life is governed by something outside my control.*

"I can't do that. I just don't have the time." *"Something outside me—limited time—is controlling me".*

"If only my wife were more patient." *Someone else's behavior is limiting my effectiveness.*

"I have to do it." *Circumstances or other people are forcing me to do what I do. I'm not free to choose my own actions.*

That language comes from a basic paradigm of determinism. And the whole spirit of it is the transfer of responsibility. *I am not responsible, not able to choose my response.* (1989, p. 78)

Fundamentally imbedded in the reactive thinking syndrome, where the password is "I-am-not-responsible" thinking, will be considerable "if-only" language. If only the economy were better, if only we had more team players, if only my boss were person-centered and not task-centered, if only I didn't have all this paperwork, if only this, if only that. **Excuses, excuses, and more excuses!** It is poisonous, self limited, handicapped, victimized thinking. It is a monkey on the back of the corporate structure, and it must be driven away if we expect to get results.

Entitlement As a Way of Thinking

Wherever there are excuses, there—if we poke around a bit—we will invariably find hiding an attitude of "entitlement." In Judith Bardwick's provocative book _Danger in the Comfort Zone_, she writes:

Entitlement is the name I have given to an attitude, a way of looking at life. Those who have this attitude believe that they do not have to earn what they get. They come to believe that they get something because they are owed it because they are _entitled_ to it. They get what they want because of _who_ they are, not because of what they _do_.

Entitlement is what I have been seeing in American corporations: people not really contributing, but still expecting to get their regular raise, their scheduled promotion...Entitlement destroys motivation. It lowers productivity. In the long run it crushes self-esteem...is epidemic in this country. (1991, p.3)

And later she adds:

We are more likely to sustain Entitlement in people when...we see [them] as victim[s]. (1991, p. 153)

Here it is again: excuses in the making. When people think in "victim" terms, they believe they are freed from having to take responsibility. They are entitled to _whatever_ simply because it is owed to them, not because they've earned it. And once things are owed to them, excuses _must_ follow. There is no other possibility. It goes with the territory. "I shouldn't have to do this or that in order to get what I want. I am entitled to it."

Entitlement thinking is logic in itself. It swims in the same stream of logic with reactive thinking, victimization, and **excuses, excuses, excuses.** It is too often *the* American corporate logic. It's what Dr. Bardwick calls in her subtitle "the habit that's killing American business."

Where there are excuses, there will be undesirable results! The habit of excuse-making is the habit that is breeding entitlement thinking. It is the same habit that is killing American business!

The Projection of Blame

Wherever there are excuses, there—if we poke around a bit—we will invariably find hiding the projection of blame. Implicitly or explicitly, projection of blame is a partner of excuse-making. Remember George, whose report was due at the March meeting. It wasn't his fault—he was just too busy (in addition to procrastination, *projection of blame* onto busyness). So he passed it on to Frank. It must have been Frank's fault (*projection of blame* onto Frank). Of course, Frank was too busy (*projection of blame* onto Frank's busyness). And so it goes. It is always easier to blame our behavior on someone or something other than ourselves. Remember what we said in Chapter 4 about pain and trying to avoid it? Blaming our shortcomings on ourselves is painful. Projecting blame onto others is relatively painless, as well as automatic, instantaneous, and predictable. And not easily changed unless that change is planned.

And Much More

We could go on at considerable length pursuing similar hidden connections. For example, wherever there is blame, there we will invariably find hiding an abundance of externalization ("Johnny made me do it"). Where there is externalization, there we will find hiding an abundance of can't-do thinking ("I can't do that because..."). Where there is can't-do thinking, there we will find hiding an abundance of irresponsibility. Where there is irresponsibility, there we will invariably find little, if any, accountability. Wherever there is no accountability, there we will find helpless thinking, self-deceit, mistrust, hidden motives, etc., etc., etc.

It would not be difficult to further unravel each of these scenarios—just as we have done with victimization, procrastination, reactive thinking, entitlement, and the projection of blame-to show that excuses are the common denominator of every major problem in corporate America. We won't, however, because we hope by now the point is clear. **Excuses are an indicator of most—if not all—of the chronic problems in corporate America. Where we find excuses, we will always find some combination of the others. They all lurk in the larger body of the iceberg that is hidden beneath the surface of the water. Each of them points to the presence of all the others. They go together in ways that are almost impossible to separate. If we have one, we have them all, in varying degrees. Taken collectively, they make it almost impossible to get the results we are looking to achieve!**

What are these chronic corporate problems that excuses are always in the middle of? The following diagram reveals some of the more common behaviors and problems that hide beneath the presence of excuses—each of which significantly interferes with the accomplishment of desired results.

Figure 3

The Enemy Is Elusive

The point is that these various blights on American companies are bacteria of a similar strain. They are cousins that travel together. Where you find one, you are

45

likely to find many others, if not all.

Which leads us to the *second* reason why we see the elimination of excuse-making as so vitally important to the cure for our corporate ailments. It has to do with the difficulty, the frustration, the futility of trying to get a grip on such things as victimization, helplessness, procrastination, reactive thinking, irresponsibility, accountability, entitlement, and the like. They are—like a marine recruit's hair after the first cut—nearly impossible to get a hold of. The same is not true, however, about excuses. Once recognized, they can be quantified, measured, remedied, and eliminated. Excuses are real and tangible things. They can be taken hold of while the problems they point to tend to elude our grasp. Yet by getting a grip on excuses, we can get a stranglehold on every problem that perplexes our companies! Excuses can be fixed! And wonderful outcomes occur—that is, the other problems go away—when the proper machinery is set into place for a company to be able to follow the maxim: *No Excuses in the Workplace!*

In Summary

We have seen that there is a way of thinking that has gradually, insidiously, silently, and methodically crept its way into the mainstream of American thinking. It is an attitude that has many faces, most of which lie beneath the surface of awareness in the same way that most of an iceberg lies beneath the surface of the water.

Despite the many elusive forms and figures this family of problems can twist and bend itself into, there is one that is distinguishable above all the others. It is one that we *can* get a clear look at (though we must *learn* to see it, since it takes a unique vantage point to do so). It is one that is possible to get a firm hold on. That one, of course, is **excuse-making**.

Excuse-making is *the* major roadblock to achieving the outcomes we desire. The longer we fail to recognize it, the longer we wait to get a firm grip on it, the longer it goes unattended, the more problematic it becomes in terms of getting the results we want.

One Last Thought

We have shown how many of the problems that perplex our companies today tend to travel together, like wolves in a pack. We have further touched on how one of those problems, namely excuse-making, gives us access to *the entire family of problems* in ways that none of the others can, Excuse-making is like the lead wolf in the pack. It shows first.

What we haven't yet looked at in any detail, however, is a unique quality about excuses that allows us to exterminate the whole family by eliminating just one of its members. That is, when we get rid of excuses, we have not just shot the lead wolf. Rather, we have blown up the entire family of problems, both the visible *and* hidden parts, and thereby have annihilated the complete pack!

Let's therefore take a closer look at how it's possible to eliminate all of the troublesome relatives of excuse making in one fell swoop by simply eliminating excuses. After that we will head into "Part II." The Scope of the Problem: How Excuses Manifest Themselves in Corporations.

CHAPTER 6

Kill Many Birds with a Single Stone

It is generally true that what we think about **X** determines how we functiun in relation to **X**. That is to say, our beliefs define the parameters within which we are able to take action. How we see something defines and limits what we can do. For example:

Beliefs of Old No. I

There was a time in the course of human history when it was commonly believed that the world was flat. That belief defined and limited our choices regarding how to be at sea. Man would venture out on the water only so far as land remained visible. Then he reversed his course and returned home. He was afraid that if he sailed any farther away from the shore, he would fall—off the edge of the earth, never to be heard from again. His behavior was consistent with, and limited by, the beliefs he held about the world *at that time.*

Beliefs of Old No. 2

It was only a little more than 100 years ago when those who demonstrated "abnormal" behavior were thought to be possessed by the devil. Such behaviors as drunkenness, infidelity, or sudden outbursts of emotion were handled in ways that today would be considered barbaric and inhumane. Some of the customary treatments were whipping, lowering slowly into poisonous snakepits, forced feedings of a mixture of sheep manure and wine, public ridicule, noise-making, and unexpected icy baths. The objective was always the same—to "scare the devil" out of a person, a saying that remains with us today. Our behavior for dealing with people who acted abnormally, though perfectly logical given the frame through which we viewed it, was limited by our way of thinking about abnormal behavior *at that time.*

Beliefs of Old No. 3

During the Industrial Revolution, children worked long, hard hours—12 and 14 hour days—in the emerging industrial plants. If children were forced to labor by those same standards today, we would consider it unusually cruel and abusive treatment. Yet such behavior was common place then because it was consistent with the beliefs about the role of children in the family. It was a value that carried over from the farmlands where for centuries children had been expected to work long hours in the fields to help support the family. The forced employment of the young was defined, and limited, by the beliefs about the role of children *at that time.*

More Recently

We need not look so far into the past to see this same principle at work. Consider the issue of women in the workplace. It was popularly believed by many in the past, and by some yet today, that a woman's place is in the home. Let's go back a mere twenty years. Only 3 percent of the attorneys in this country in 1972 were women. In addition, it was nearly unthinkable for a woman to travel overnight. It was believed that if she did, the other men's wives would be jealous and would not tolerate it. So as a general rule, women didn't travel overnight. Our behavior was limited and defined by the beliefs that we held.

Today, the beliefs about women in the workplace have changed considerably, and therefore, so have our behaviors. In 1993, forty-one percent of the practicing attorneys and forty-seven percent of the enrollees in law school were women. Furthermore, women travel overnight as common practice in the business community. *Beliefs set the parameters on our behavior, on how we do things, on how we function. Simply put,* **we are limited by what we believe.**

Athletic records furnish many interesting examples. When it was believed impossible for an individual to run one mile in four minutes or less, runners mostly didn't challenge that belief. Their behavior was consistent within the accepted paradigm. The goal was to *approach* four minutes, but *exceed* it? Never! And then came Roger Bannister, a man who believed differently. Through his belief that a four-minute mile *was* possible, the limits of his behavior were expanded, new possibilities arose, and new horizons were reached. And now to run one mile in four minutes, though still a tremendous feat, is nevertheless fairly common.

And so it is with every new world record, every new invention, and every new technique that betters the old way of doing *anything*. **All progress begins with a belief that something can be better, a mental framework that sees it differently from the accepted and customary way of seeing it, a perspective that is out of the ordinary.**

Perception Affects Reality

The point is that it has been true throughout the course of human history, and it will probably always be true, that our view—our perception—of anything determines the limits within which we can, and will, deal with that thing. Our behavior is, generally speaking, logical and consistent within the context of the lens through which we are looking. Change the lens, the paradigm, the mindset, the belief system, and amazing new opportunities arise.

When we were able to perceive the world as round rather than flat, whole new horizons opened up for world travel. When we changed our view that abnormal behavior was caused by mental and emotional factors rather than by demon possession, new and effective opportunities for treating the mentally ill emerged. When we changed our perception of the role of children in the family, tremendous new strides were made in our definitions of fair treatment and education of the young.

Re-examining the Lens

Similarly, the time has arrived in the course of corporate development to update and upgrade the lens through which we are accustomed to looking at problems in the workplace. Our experience continues to demonstrate that the current paradigms are not as effective as they might be. They are often too narrow and too limited to fix the problems that have a stronghold in organizational structures today. This book is about a shift to a powerful new way of looking at corporate problems, and the amazing new possibilities that such a shift opens up for fixing those problems.

Relationships Between Things

There are three ways to view the relationship between any two or more things. The relationship might be **causal,** it might be **coincidental,** or it might be **mutually coexistent,** also known as **systemic.** While the distinctions between these may appear at first glance to be a bit academic, it is very important to understand their differences in order to **(1) grasp the basic premise of this book,** and **(2) use these concepts to fix your company's problems.**

Causal Relationships

A causal relationship is one in which something (the cause) sets in motion something else (the effect). Eye strain causes headaches. Viruses and bacteria cause infections. Poorly maintained equipment causes shutdowns. Shutdowns cause loss in production. Ineffective management causes low levels of human performance. All of these are examples of cause and effect relationships. Headaches are related to eye strain *causally*, equipment breakdown is related to poor maintenance *causally*, etc. In simple terms, one thing causes the other to happen.

Coincidental Relationships

A coincidental relationship is one in which something is related to something else by chance. There is no particular rhyme or reason why something happened in a certain way; it just happened. A car passes another car on the expressway. The relationship between the two cars is coincidental. It just happened that way. The director of computer operations is out of town on the same day that the system breaks down. The relationship between the two events is coincidental.

Mutually Coexistent (Systemic) Relationships

When the relationship between two or more things is mutually coexistent, they are related neither causally nor coincidentally. That is, one does not cause the other, nor are they related by some chance happening. They simply go together as parts of the same system. Arms don't _cause_ hands and fingers, nor is it merely a coincidence that where we find one, we also find the others. They are part of a system where one part "goes with" the others. They are mutually coexistent. Porcupines don't _cause_ their quills, and the relationship between porcupines and quills is not just by chance. Quills simply "gowith" porcupines. They are part of the package. Managers don't _cause_ workers, nor are they related by chance. Management and labor go together. They cannot be separated. So with trees and leaves, heads and tails, up and down. All of these things are examples of mutually coexistent relationships—things that "go with" other things. Coexistent relationships are those where something exists as part of something else, mutually, necessarily, **systemically.**

The Current Corporate Paradigms

Traditionally, we have looked at and analyzed problems in the corporate world either through the lens of cause/effect, or through the lens of coincidence. In the first case, we have viewed this or that problem as being caused by something, and then we have set about trying to change that thing (the cause). For example, if we think that the problem of diminishing productivity is caused by inadequate teamwork, the usual method of fixing the problem is to try to build better teams. If shrinking sales is *caused* by poorly trained salespeople, then the solution is generally either to hire trained salespeople or train the old ones. This is far and away the most commonly used paradigm for analyzing and fixing corporate problems. It is the accepted corporate perspective.

We also tend to view some corporate problems as coincidental. That is, some problems pop up here and there, not from any obvious causation, but more or less by chance. In a sense, causal and coincidental explanations are closely related, the only real difference being whether or not we think we can identify the cause of some event. When we can, we use causal explanations. When we can't, we tend to see it as a coincidence.

For example, Sam in accounting is irritable and argues often with his assistant, Adam. There is some possibility that we'd look for departmental stressors as a cause of that problem, but more often we're likely to see Sam as short fused, someone who "just hasn't been himself lately". Either fix Sam or tolerate him. This is an example of coincidental analysis of problems. The problematic situation appears to be isolated and unrelated to other things. When this is the case, the fix is usually *very* narrow in focus, even more so than with remedies based on causal explanations.

A New Way of Seeing the Problem

By themselves, these traditional ways of looking at corporate problems are inadequate and outdated. Limiting our analysis to cause/effect and coincidence explanations is analogous to thinking the world is flat, or that the patent office should close because all that can be invented has been invented. They can vastly limit exciting new opportunities for fixing the problems.

It is our experience that the stubborn problems in corporate America today can be most effectively addressed and resolved by looking through the lens of mutual co-existence as an explanatory model. It is our view that most of the problems in organizations today "gowith" other problems. Attempting to resolve those problems through cause-and-effect or coincidence models will nearly always fall short for the same reason that dropping people unexpectedly into icy baths didn't solve the problem of abnormal behavior. The paradigm doesn't fit the reality of the situation.

The secret—the key to the vault that holds the treasure—is to seek out the family of problems that travel together as a *system*. Having done that, the next step is to identify and isolate the part (or parts) that most affect the other parts that "go with" it. If this can be done, then the task is to choke off that one essential component that governs all the others until one by one the other parts perish. It is rather like cutting off the head of a chicken. The chicken will run around for a few seconds as if still alive once its head is severed. But all of the parts that "gowith" that component—its legs, wings, feet, heart, lungs, etc.—soon die without the essential part, the head.

Excuses: The Essential Part

This book is about severing the head from a whole body of problems in corporate America so that, one by one, all of the problems will die. Our experience has taught us that the head of the chicken in terms of corporate problems is **excuse-making.** It more than any other single factor indicates, perpetuates, and dominates other problems in the workplace. It is the one common denominator of the troubles that perplex our organizations. By isolating and eliminating this single phenomenon, all the other problems that accompany it are rendered impotent. Let's change our analogy of the iceberg with all of its underwater components to that of a buoyant mine, the kind that blows up ships on contact. Let's say, also, that the trigger points that explode the mine are excuses.

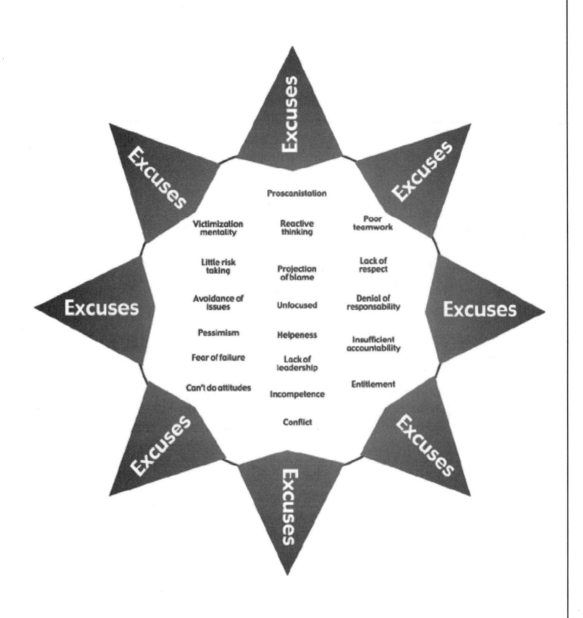

Figure 4

If we remove the spikes, the trigger points, from the mine, there would be nothing to set the mine off. It would be harmless, just another small object floating in the water.

Since there would be no way for the explosives to be denotated, every other corporate troublemaker would be rendered inert.

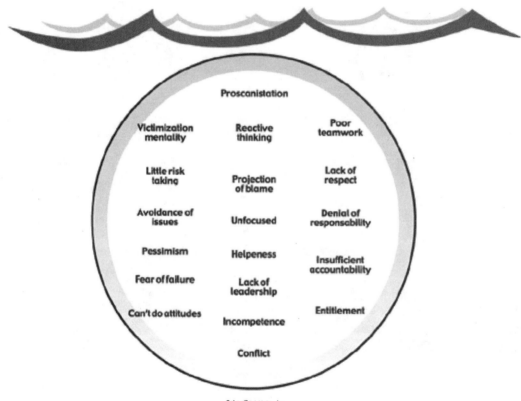

Proscanistation

Victimization mentality

Reactive thinking

Poor teamwork

Little risk taking

Projection of blame

Lack of respect

Avoidance of issues

Unfocused

Denial of responsability

Pessimism

Helpeness

Insufficient accountability

Fear of failure

Lack of leadership

Can't do attitudes

Incompetence

Entitlement

Conflict

Figure 5

We will explore in some detail why this is the case—that the same stone that removes excuses from the workplace kills all of the other pesky "birds" that go with them, as well. And we will examine closely what comprises the bigger family of problems to be eliminated.

As you are about to see, *most,* if not all, of the problems that perplex the corporate world today are members of that family of birds. And for the first time, there is a systemic approach that will wipe out *all* of the problems, not just one here and one there, as has been true in the past.

————◦◦◦ ▷◉◁ ◦◦◦————

When you eliminate excuses, *you get rid of all the other problems. When you get rid of the other problems, you make room for the positives. When you make room for the positives,* **you get results!**

Traditional Strategies

It will also become clearer as we go along why the traditional methods of addressing the problems in our companies do not produce long-term improvements. Consulting and training programs that approach the solution through conventional cause-and-effect or coincidence paradigms usually *cannot* effect any lasting change. How could they? It would be like filing down the claws of a tiger who had just clawed someone to death. The fix would be temporary because claws grow back; and it would be ineffective anyway because there are other ways a tiger can kill people. The point is that when corporate problems are addressed from a cause-and-effect paradigm, there generally can only be a series of shifts in the system, and it isn't long before the old problems recur.

Furthermore, even when we do try to fix problems in organizations through cause-and-effect approaches, we usually try to fix the people first. We tend to think that if we just had very talented people (cause), the problems will be solved (effect). So what do we do? We try to make superstars, extraordinary people, and we bring in all kinds of trainers and consultants to make this happen. But listen to Peter Schutz, former CEO of Porsche AG.

The secret of success in business rarely consists of finding a group of superstars. The secret actually lies in getting extraordinary performance out of ordinary people. What makes an extraordinary person is an extraordinary organization, and an extraordinary process.

We submit to you that the way to have an extraordinary organization and an extraordinary process is to break out of the cocoon of cause-and-effect and coincidental thinking, and fly high with the wings of systemic thinking.

We are not saying, nor would we want to be mistaken to mean, that some of the time-honored programs out there such as total quality management, leadership training, interpersonal communications, sales training, trust building, team building, empowerment, and the like are unimportant or totally ineffective. *Certainly they are not.* It is more a matter of timing and integration. To attack any problem while looking through a lens that doesn't properly focus on that problem is like trying to see Mt. Everest through a microscope. It just doesn't work! Once properly focused, there most assuredly is a place for some of the traditional programs. Again, the problem is not with the corrective measures taken to date, but with the cause-and-effect perspective from which they almost always approach the problem.

We realize that the concept that it is important to look at problems from a different point of view is not new. What is new, however, is the discovery of this *powerful systemic perspective from which to look of corporate problems.* It is powerful because *it works to get results!* It works to get results because it elicits extraordinary performance from ordinary people. Therein lies the future of corporate success.

PART II

The Scope
of the Problem

How Excuses Manifest
Themselves
in Corporations

CHAPTER 7

In the Corporate Culture

Nearly everywhere you turn in corporate America these days, someone is talking about "corporate culture". And well they should be. The concept of culture is more than just current and fashionable. It is positioned critically in the center of all that is unhealthy about our companies today. If the corporations in this country are going to compete and win in the global marketplace, we must become acutely aware of the seriousness of the cultural issues that exist in our organizations. The heart and soul of the message to be learned and applied from this book rests in the very center of the cultural issue. To put it bluntly, what you're about to read is the guts of what you need to pay attention to.

What exactly is this thing that we refer to as "corporate culture"?

Definition

Cor-po-rate Cul-ture—The spoken and unspoken in an organization that set the standards for how things are to be done. The company ethos. The characteristic ways of thinking, feeling, and behaving in any given occupational group. The prevailing attitudes, values, beliefs, and actions of the people within a company.

In Other Words

All companies have a culture whether they know it or not. That is, every place of business has its characteristic ways of thinking, valuing, making decisions, and behaving. Whatever these standards are determine how people look at situations, interpret information, communicate, and act. Culture even sets the emotional tone, or feeling state, by which people function within that organization.

Corporate culture is, in effect, the personality of the company. Like people, corporations have different personalities. There are some companies where if you stand in front of the door at five o'clock you're likely to be trampled. There are other companies where people filter out slowly over the course of two or three hours. In some companies people address each other formally, in others informally. There are some companies where the work pace is quite intense and others where it is fairly relaxed. You can often sense the personality of a corporate culture from the atmosphere when yon first walk in the door. Some corporate environments are light and fun-loving, others serious and professional, even intimidating. Some inspire confidence, some don't. Some are electric and draw people, making them feel welcome. Others are boring; still others are cold and unfriendly. Some companies respond to calls from their customers with nothing but excuses. Other companies meet their customers only with solutions.

How Does It Happen?

What makes a company's culture what it is? How can one company's culture be so different from another's?

The Role of Tradition

Tradition plays a large part, not only in establishing corporate culture, but also in perpetuating it. When Nick was hired as an accountant in a large western furniture company, he was told that he was expected to report to work by 8:00 every morning. He noticed when he read the policy manual that it said the same thing. His first day on the job, Nick arrived at 7:45 a.m., happy to be in his new position and eager to get started. He couldn't help but notice, however, that the four other accountants in his department arrived between 8:30 and 9:00. Nick was a bit puzzled, but didn't think too much of it until the same pattern continued for several weeks. By the end of the first month, Nick found himself arriving at work around 8:15 a.m. He was nervous about it at first, but was relieved when nothing was said. Now, of course, after several months on the job, Nick arrives between 8:30 and 9:00 along with his colleagues.

In countless similar ways, the tireless voice of tradition speaks loudly in carrying on the culture of any company. And the problem is not just that the cultural values get passed on from one employee to another over a period of years. What's equally important is that companies tend to hire people who fit naturally into their present culture. Like attracts like. The result is that hiring people of a *similar* bent serves to feed the prevailing culture, since all such hirees will, to varying degrees, bring with them the same values that are already reflected in the company.

Taking a Broader View

An attempt to get a handle on what corporate culture is all about inclines one toward taking too narrow a view. People are used to associating culture with the framed mission statements, company slogans, motivational sayings, and handbooks that are visible around the workplace. Equally, corporate culture is thought of as whatever people in the workplace say it is. *Culture is much, much more than what is framed, written, or spoken about in a company.* Culture consists also of all that is unframed, unwritten, and unspoken. In fact, just as in Nick's company, **corporate culture is *mostly* what is unframed, unwritten, and unspoken.**

Let's explore more closely what we mean by looking at a few examples.

Reactivity vs. Proactivity

Very few people today would take issue with the notion that it is important to be proactive in business—to make things happen rather than wait for them to happen.

Many gurus on the subject, including Stephen Covey, have done an excellent job of helping companies become aware of how important proactivity really is. But our experience in the corporate world continues suggest that any actual implementation of the concept of proactivity too often stops at the level of precept. That is, proactivity is a wonderful *rule* to believe in. It is a profound maxim for governing corporate conduct. Not uncommonly, CEO's, corporate executives, and managers stand in front of their people and preach the message of proactivity. "We want this company to be more proactive! If we don't become more proactive, we may not be around in five years." Some company leaders strongly recommend reading certain books on the subject. Others buy copies for everyone in management and make it mandatory reading. (Not a bad idea, really.)

The problem is that *saying you believe in* proactivity, suggesting that people read the latest best-seller about it, and even making proactivity a formal written part of our corporate culture will not by themselves make people more proactive. *You must also change what they do, since it is the* **behavior** *of your people that defines your culture.* It doesn't matter how much you persuade your people to *believe in* proactivity, for example, if—in their behavior—they remain more focused on short-term goals than on long-term goals. If they are focused on short-term goals, they are probably in more of a reactive mindset than a proactive one, *regardless of what you'd have them believe about proactivity.*

Warren Bennis in his book *On Becoming a Leader* quotes television producer and writer Norman Lear as saying that short-term thinking is "the societal disease of our time." Why? Because when we are focused on the short term, we rarely take into consideration the long-term consequences of our decisions and our behaviors. And those long-term consequences could be very damaging.

Bennis agrees with Lear. He thinks that short-term thinking is seriously holding back business in this country. Listen to his words:

> *I think Lear is absolutely right. American business has become the principal shaper and mover in contemporary America—even more than television—and has, in an odd irony, by zealously practicing what it preaches, sandbagged itself. Having captured the heart and mind of the nation with its siren songs and instant gratification, it has locked itself into obsolete practices. American business has never been more popular and less successful. . . Dick Ferry, president and cofounder of Korn/Ferry, agrees, and he is not optimistic. "Corporate America may talk, on an intellectual level, about what it'll take to succeed in the twenty-first century, but when it gets right down to decision making, all that matters is the next quarterly earnings report. That's what's driving much of the system. With that mind-set, everything else*

becomes secondary to the ability to deliver the next quarterly earnings push-up. We're on a treadmill. The reward system in this country is geared to the short term." (1989, p.22-23).

Again, *corporate culture is mostly what is unframed, unwritten, and unspoken.* If the people in your company are more focused on the short term almost to the exclusion of the long term, the corporate culture is one of **reactivity**, not proactivity, regardless of what everyone would like to think to the contrary!

An Example of How This Works

Long-term strategic planning for one's job is an exercise in proactivity. When was the last time you saw an evaluation form or appraisal process that gave any credit to the employee for being able to do long-term strategic planning? Usually, the evaluation process focuses on how well the person handled some specific assignment or duty in the short term.

If you want to improve *anything,* you have to measure it. How can we measure proactivity when little attempt is made to quantify what it is that constitutes proactivity? Let's say you want your salespeople to "proactively" seek larger accounts. So you ask them to do market research on large companies before going in. That way they will know what the company is all about and they will impress the potential customer as being well-prepared and well-informed. This would be an example of proactive selling.

Clearly, to actively seek larger accounts is a long term process. You can't just have your people throw aside everything they're doing and tell them to spend the next three months researching big clients in order to go out and make the calls. In addition, you can expect that this will take them out of their emotional comfort zones and cause considerable distress. So your people need to be taught how to blend this proactive project into their weekly goals program and their weekly accountabilities program.

Ask them to identify perhaps four major accounts they want to land in the next year. Then have them set up benchmark measuring points for the year to determine their progress in terms of specific goals—doing research, action plans, etc.. These goals are then built into their accountabilities system, and so on. More about this later.

Similarly, when was the last time you saw a sales professional's appraisal in which one of the appraisal issues involved **(a) how well this person developed his sales plan, (b) how well he followed his sales plan, and (c) whether his sales plan used creativity and proactivity to attack the market?** These are things we rarely look at to evaluate. If we aren't going to evaluate them, how can we expect our people to perform to those standards? *As long as our evaluations and accountabilities are set up on a short-term basis, we're not going to have a proactive corporate culture, no matter what is said at the meetings, no matter what books are recommended, and no matter how the mission statement reads.* Short-term thinking and proactivity are contradictory concepts.

The Same Example Extended

So here is Larry, a better-than-average salesman for eight years with a leading computer software company. The company has had shrinking profit margins for the past two years, and the CEO is concerned. He knows that something must change. He recently attended a week-long workshop that emphasized, among other things, the importance of salespeople's proactivity in the marketplace. He discovered that being more forward-looking was necessary not only to get ahead, but maybe even just to survive.

The CEO returned, excited about what he had learned. He called a meeting of his regional sales managers. Who in turn called meetings with their respective salespeople, to sell them on the idea of becoming more proactive. He handed out a popular book on the subject to everyone. He insisted that the words "BE PROACTIVE" be made into some attractive posters and placed generously around the workplace in clear view of everyone. He even appointed a committee of top managers to re-examine the company's mission statement and build the concept of proactivity into it.

Larry was inspired. His CEO and his sales manager both did an exceptional job of impressing on him the importance of this new approach. At first, Larry's excitement was expressed in the form of some new-found energy in making his sales calls. He had a one-month and three-month sales quota to meet, and he was fired up about it. Little more was said to him about becoming proactive by the CEO and sales manager until the next semi-annual sales meeting, at which time the company's "buy-in" to the concept of proactivity was restated and reinforced in the various speeches given by management.

Nothing else changed. There was no effort to build proactivity into Larry's goals, evaluations, or accountabilities. The demands placed on him to meet short-term quotas soon overshadowed any excitement he might have had for becoming proactive. Larry did the best he could to be more proactive, at least by his limited understanding of the whole notion. Mostly, in retrospect, what proactivity meant to him was to actually do what was expected of him rather than to put things off. Since the whole concept was never clearly explained in detailed, practical terms, nor built into his accountabilities in a way that could be measured, Larry was not able to meet the "proactive" expectations of his superiors. "Proactivity" became a precept to believe in, but it had no meaningful behavioral significance.

And It Fails

As could be expected, the whole proactive agenda was lost in the flurry of short-term activities. So what? Consider the possible consequences. At the end of the fiscal year when the company profits have further fallen, will Larry be more likely to accept the blame or project it onto someone or something else? Will his attitude be more optimistic or pessimistic about the next management strategy that comes along? Will he be respectful of his superiors, or disrespectful, especially if the CEO places a good chunk of the blame for shrinking profits on the sales force for not being proactive enough? Would the resulting stress in the sales department express itself as conflict between Larry and his colleagues? Will Larry feel like he has the power to change things, to make things happen? Or will he feel like a victim? What if he didn't quite make his one-month and three-month quotas because he was, in fact, spending some of his time doing long-term, proactive planning? Would he be rewarded for that behavior, or would he be punished? If he were punished, would he tend to become more positive in his sales efforts, or more negative?

More to the point. **Here come the excuses:** "Larry, why didn't you reach your monthly goal?" "It's been a tough month, sir." "Larry, what have you done to become more proactive in the market place?" "I've tried to do more reading at night, sir, to become more informed about product knowledge when I'm with a customer." "Larry, this company is sinking, fast. What can you do to help?" "I'll try harder next month, sir." "Larry, I notice that your attitude has been slipping. You've been really negative lately." "Things have been rough at home recently, sir." "Larry, what's the problem between you and your colleague Steve?" "He's been hard to get along with lately, sir." "Larry, why wasn't your last monthly report submitted on time?" "I've been very busy trying to be more proactive, sir."

One reason people don't get results is because they are *allowed* to make excuses. Another reason people don't get results is because they are *encouraged*—almost "forced" by the system—to make excuses. **When the system is set up in such a way that failure is inevitable, excuse-making is unknowingly encouraged in that company.** This is because, given the choice between admitting to failure or making an excuse, most people, most of the time will automatically give an excuse to spare themselves the pain. Again, excuses are an indicator, a warning signal, of a systemic problem (or problems) in the company. Where there are excuses, there—if we poke around a bit—we will find hiding other problems. Excuses never travel alone.

The Arithmetic Factor

Now multiply this one simple example about Larry by the entire work force of 239, or 1800, or however many people are in the corporation, and you have what is commonplace in our companies: **an excuse-laden corporate culture.** Again, it is not a question of *whether* excuse-making happens (since virtually every business is infected to some degree), but *how much* does it happen? Those companies where excuses are the most commonplace are the ones that are in the most trouble. Those companies where excuse-making happens the least are leading their respective industries.

The Point

Always, **when you don't get results, you get excuses.** _And you can't get results unless the desired outcome is purposely and carefully built into the evaluation and accountabilities process._ A long-term, proactive approach often requires the acceptance of possible short-term sacrifice. No amount of corporate-culture preaching or propaganda, no fancy posters or motivational plaques, no eloquent speeches at national sales meetings will eliminate excuses from the workplace—_unless_ the desired behaviors (and reasonable expectations) are built into the appraisal process. **But as long as there are excuses, there will not be results!**

The Problem Is Systemic

It is important to note that, though our first example was about reactivity vs. proactivity, we could have started with any behavioral problem listed in the base of the iceberg (figure 5) and arrived eventually at the same place, namely, the excuse-making process. For example, and in a much less detailed way, let's look at pessimism vs. optimism. Pessimism is one of the ingredients that is at the core of cultural issues. How can you have proactivity if you're not optimistic? Optimism is about the future; pessimism is rooted in the past. How can you be focused, or have good teamwork, or take risks, or trust, or have harmonious relationships, or lead, or feel empowered, or not fear failure, or stretch yourself to meet commitments, if you are pessimistic? And now the key. _Pessimistic people will always be making excuses. Optimistic people rarely make excuses. There lies one of the important control factors._ **We won't eliminate pessimism in the workplace unless or until we get rid of excuses!**

Why? Again, wherever there is short-term thinking there is reactivity. Wherever there is reactivity, there is the lack of stretching to keep commitments. Wherever there is lack of stretching to keep commitments, there will be little risk-taking. Where there is little risk-taking, there will be fear of failure. Where there is fear of failure, there will be "can't do" attitudes. Where there are "can't-do" attitudes, there will be victimization. Wherever there is victimization, there will be helplessness. And where there is helplessness, there will be pessimism and procrastination. Where there is procrastination, there will be the loss of creativity. And where there is loss of creativity, there will be following instead of leading. Where there is following instead of leading, there will be denial of responsibility. And where there is denial of responsibility, there will be *excuse-making,* just as surely as the sun will come up tomorrow.

And So On

To make the point as clear as possible, we used one example about reactive thinking, and another about pessimism. Notice how the issues began to overlap one another. This is the way it is with tracking any negative characteristic in a corporate culture. The real problem is systemic in nature, so no matter where you begin, you soon return to the place where you started. It is like the circumference of a circle. No matter where you start, your journey will always take you back to the point of departure.

Furthermore, as you make the journey around the circumference, if you look to the inside of the circle, the midpoint will always be the same. It is the stake in the ground from which all points on the circle are determined. So does every negative corporate culture have a midpoint from which all the characteristics of a negative culture can be measured. That midpoint is, always, excuse-making.

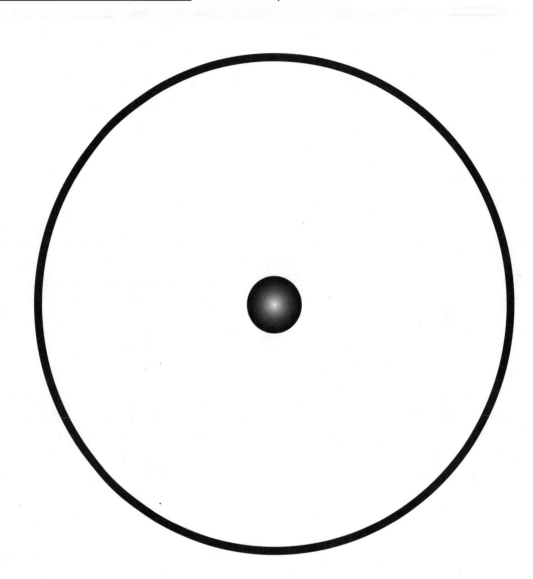

Figure 6

Figure 7

Because excuses are at the midpoint, they are of central importance. They may or may not show while their cousins hide, and vice versa. But just as with a circle, if there were no midpoint, there would be no circle. Similarly, if there were no excuses, there would be no more negative culture. It would be gone, in one fell swoop! The remedy, the *cure,* the fix that really works and actually lasts, is to develop a corporate culture—not just in word, but *in deed*—where there are no excuses in the workplace!

In Review

- Understanding the concept of corporate culture is instrumental to fixing the problems that exist in our organizations.

- Every company has a culture. Usually, that culture is much more than what people in the organization think it is. Culture involves all the subtle rules of how to think, feel, and behave in a company. For most organizations, this involves much that is not said, not written, and not framed on a plaque.

- Tradition plays a large role in passing culture on to the next generation. Corporate behavior perpetuates itself.

- Many companies have excuse-laden cultures. Then context in which excuses abound consists of many negative characteristics that point to one another, each of which are poisonous to the overall effectiveness of the company.

- These poisons include, among others denial of responsibility, projection of blame, procrastination, reactive thinking, self-deceit, pessimism, victimization thinking, entitlement attitudes, and the refusal to be accountable.

- Sometimes excuses are evident and these other problems tend to be hidden. Sometimes it is just the opposite: excuses are difficult to recognize while their relatives are not. A valuable rule of thumb is. *(1) If you detect any of the above poisons in your company, you can be sure there are excuses; and (2) If you detect excuses, you can be sure the other poisons are there, too.* The problem is systemic; excuses and their relatives "go with" each other.

- If you want results, then excuses must go. By ridding yourself of this one corporate ailment, all the related problems—the poisons—are also cleaned out of the system. The result will be not merely a surviving but a thriving business. And you will be well on the way to becoming number one again!

Notes and Quotes

It is easy to make excuses when we ought to be making opportunities.

Warren Wiersbe

CHAPTER 8

In Leadership

Leadership has never been such a hot topic in corporate America. It ranks at the top of the list of developmental programs on which organizations are currently investing large sums of money. Why? Because there is a desperate need for more effective leadership in our ailing companies. Warren Bennis again:

A few years ago, a scientist at the University of Michigan listed what he considered to be the ten basic dangers to our society. First and most significant is the possibility of some kind of nuclear war or accident that would destroy the human race. The second danger is the prospect of a worldwide epidemic, disease, famine, or depression. The third of the scientist's key problems that could bring about the destruction of society is the quality of the management and leadership of our institutions. (1989, p. 14)

Leadership is the cornerstone of the whole improvement concept. Leadership is where all progress begins. Without the proper leadership, all of our institutions are in serious trouble.

What Is the Problem?

The problem is not that there is an alarming shortage of good, strong people in leadership positions in our corporations. There are plenty. The problem has more to do with how "leadership" has been understood, or more precisely, misunderstood. The tendency in most American businesses has been to see leadership as equivalent to management and administration. This is a huge mistake, as we will discuss in detail later on. The point here is that our misconceptions about leadership have played a major role in causing our middle-of-the-pack performance in world competition.

The problem is that as long as we have an outdated understanding about what constitutes an effective leader, we will continue to invest in obsolete remedies. It would be like investing our money in surgical knives if we still believed that the best cure for infection was to bleed people. The cure is not to keep replaying the old solutions, but to see the problem in a new way. So in this chapter we will look at a new understanding of what true, effective leadership is.

Definition

Lead, v,—To guide or conduct by showing the way. To precede; to introduce by going first.

The Leader As an Example

Lee Lacocca, in his book *Lacocca; An Autobiography,* said it well.

Leadership means setting an example. When you find yourself in a position of leadership, people follow your every move. . . when the leader acts, people watch. So you have to be careful about everything you say and everything you do. (1984, p. 229).

Including how you handle excuses. As the leader goes, so will others follow.

We have made it clear that the winners in the corporate race will be those companies that make purging their culture of excuses an absolute top priority. This task falls directly on the shoulders of the leaders. Ultimately, it is the responsibility of the leaders to provide the impetus necessary to establish and maintain on excuse-free culture. *The definition of leadership* must *include this one, central theme. Only this kind of leadership can keep the employees of a company from regressing to the excuse-making mode, a mode—you will recall—that is built into people by nature to help them protect themselves. This understanding of leadership is the only way to regain and hold the winning edge in the current marketplace.*

Leadership Culture vs. Employee Culture

Technically speaking, a corporation cannot have a culture short of the people who make up the company. A company's culture will always be a combination of the culture of the employees and the culture of the leaders. The leaders may well not be directly responsible for causing a company's culture. Often, the corporate culture was inherited by leaders when they joined or took over the company. But always, as the leaders assume control, they are responsible for **(1) deciding what type of culture they want, (2) identifying the culture that exists, (3) deciding in what ways they want to intervene to bring the company to the desired culture, (4) implementing the developmental programs to bring the desired results, and (5) measuring the results of the intervention(s) to ensure that they are working.** Again, when this is not properly taken care of, excuses will grow as rapidly as weeds. *The company that is not working through strong leaders to avoid an excuse-making culture is a company with an excuse-laden culture. If you don't work to prevent it, you will by default end up with it.* And with the excuse-laden culture will come the whole family of excuse-related characteristics.

The First Problem

As we said, the biggest single problem about leadership in corporate America today is confusion about what constitutes a leader. Many organizations don't differentiate between leadership on the one hand, and management and administration on the other. However, management and administration are the antitheses of the concept of leadership that is required to regain pre-eminence in the global marketplace. The work of those in managerial and administrative positions is defined by their titles. Administrators administer past policy, and managers manage *existing* conditions. Certainly, these functions are important in any organization. But they are not to be equated with leadership. Leadership is futuristic by its very nature. Leaders *show the way, precede, and introduce by going first.* Leadership is, by definition, proactive. It is grounded in can-do attitudes, courage to face issues, creative thinking, empowered behavior, optimism, stretching to meet commitments, risk-taking, internalization of responsibility, and long-term focus. In other words, leadership involves excuse-free behavior.

How Is the Confusion of Management and Administration with Leadership a Problem?

In most companies, one of two things is true about the leaders. Either there is no differentiation between leaders, managers, and administrators—in which case leaders function in the same way as managers and administrators; or, if they have been differentiated, the leaders in the company *have been promoted from within the ranks* of management and administration.

An Example

Allen graduated with his MBA from a relatively unknown business college in the Northwest. At age 23 he was hired into a middle management position at a growing manufacturing company. Allen was a conscientious manager. He took his job seriously and, by and large, performed admirably in his various areas of responsibility. His managerial skills were recognized and appreciated, and he was rewarded by working his way through the usual promotion process within the company as it continued to grow. Twenty years later, Allen was offered the position of senior vice-president in charge of operations. Of course, he accepted the job. Why wouldn't be? He had worked long and hard to get there. It was the payoff for his stellar work over the years as a manager.

But what was Allen trained to do? And what was he good at doing? *Managing, period*! His skills were superb at managing existing conditions, which is what a manager does in his company. A leader, remember, is future-focused. A leader's mindset is on what is coming, and his energy goes into figuring out how to lead others into and through that maze. Allen was not trained as a leader. He did not function in any of his work experience as a leader. He did not think as a leader. In fact, he wasn't even aware of how a leader differs from a manager in job responsibility.

It is now five years later. Allen is 48 years old. What might we suppose about the profile of this company under Allen's leadership? Is the corporation likely to be on the cutting edge of innovation in its field? Is it likely to be gaining market share or losing market share? Is it proactively seeking larger accounts, or is it more focused on managing the accounts that they currently have? When projections aren't met, is Allen of the mindset to take responsibility for that, or does he hunt for the perfect scapegoat?

Allen isn't a make-believe character. He is real, and here are the facts. Every year for five consecutive years, Allen has fired one or more of the four VP's who report to him. Why? Because every year Allen would go to the CEO and make his projections on what the company profits would be – and every year the company fell short. So every year he fired at least one VP. He projected all of the blame for the company's failure onto the VP's. The first two or three years, it was easy to think there might be some validity in Allen's behavior. Now, however, after five years of the same thing over and over, Allen is in trouble. The CEO is beginning to catch on. He has stopped wondering why the company was losing good people. He sees that Allen is firing VP's because of his unwillingness or inability to admit that he's the person who is responsible for the failure(s). **Allen is making excuses!**

It Is Not Entirely Allen's Fault

Let's talk about how Allen made it through twenty years as a manager. Chances are that he did it by playing the game of corporate politics and by keeping his nose clean. Many times over those years Allen witnessed a recurring phenomenon. Some manager in the company would show a few signs of leadership by taking a risk here and there, and occasionally failing. As problems developed up the executive ladder, Allen observed that the person who took a risk was scapegoated and let go or forced out of his job. He learned quickly that the emphasis was on placing blame rather than learning from mistakes.

So you see, the Allens in corporate America don't necessarily get to the top through superior performance.

Often they get there by not taking risks, by not being proactive, by being average, by continuing to do what's been done in the past, and by learning how to stay out of harm's way. Such behavior serves to keep them out of trouble, and therefore they manage to survive while others around them take the fall. Because they have survived, they are the only ones left with any seniority. So naturally, they get the promotions.

By the time the Allens finally make it to the top, they have totally absorbed this corporate way of thinking. It is only natural, and to be expected, that they will handle problems from the top exactly as they saw them handled all the years they were coming up the corporate ladder. When problems develop that they should be taking responsibility for, they will find the necessary scapegoats and get rid of them. Typically the goats will be those individuals who have demonstrated a flair for being proactive, for making a few waves by showing some initiative, and by taking an occasional risk. Risk-takers will always have some failures, and their failures usually show. When their mistakes are visible, they unfortunately become easy to hunt down and kill.

And then we wonder, where have all the leaders gone?

So Where Is the Problem?

We've seen that the problem is not entirely with Allen. In fact, if the CEO fires Allen thinking that letting him go will solve the problem, he will likely only repeat the cycle and promote someone into that position who also came from the ranks of management. That person will likely be someone who did well as a manager, but who nonetheless has a managerial thinking pattern, just like Allen. In time, the problem can only repeat itself. This is because the problem is built into the corporate system. It is like inbreeding in a family. If one child proves to be maladapted in some way due to genetic distortions from the inbreeding, what good will it do to boot him out of the family and raise another child to replace him? The next one is likely to be maladapted, as well. And the next one. And the next one. And so on. Firing the person who manifests the symptoms is rarely the best solution. In fact, rarely is it anything other than a very temporary solution. The symptoms will repeat themselves again and again until we recognize what the real problem is and fix it.

The Formula for Corporate Victory

In the quest to become number one again, the edge will go to the companies that do whatever it takes to develop excuse-free cultures. This will happen only when we begin to train, hire, and promote people who either have leadership skills already, or who demonstrate the clear potential for developing into leaders. The difficulty has been that we've never identified what leadership skills are in relation to eliminating excuse-making from our companies. So not having identified them, we haven't been able to recognize or evaluate or foster those skills. It's just never been a goal to shoot for. But that's about to change.

The Scope of the Problem

How many Allens are there in corporate America? How many billions of dollars does it cost our companies because of all the Allens out there? How many billions more will our companies lose by allowing the problem to continue? If the current system of hiring and placing so-called leaders is allowed to continue uninterrupted, our corporations will continue to be plagued by excuse-laden cultures. And you can be absolutely sure of the following two things.

· If excuses are made and tolerated by "leaders" at the top of an organization, then excuse-making will permeate the culture from top to bottom. This is because an example has been set that excuse-making is permissable. President Truman made popular the saying, "The buck stops here." Many CEO's pride themselves by displaying a similar motto in their offices. Rarely do we think to ask, however, that if the buck stops at the top, why was it allowed to get that far up the ladder in the first

place? "Passing the buck" is nothing more than a colloquial expression for the passing of blame, the refusal to accept responsibility, and the making of excuses. "The buck stops here" implies that it doesn't stop before it gets all the way to the top. If this is true, then excuses must have been allowed. And when excuses are allowed, they will be like rats in the warehouse: For every rat you see, there are hundreds, maybe thousands, that you don't see. Similarly, for every excuse that you see at the top of an organization, there will be hundreds, maybe thousands, of excuses down the ranks of that organization that may go unnoticed. Why unnoticed? Because excuse-making is a way of thinking. It is the logic of much of corporate America. It is commonplace, and what is common goes mostly unnoticed.

· If excuses are allowed at the bottom of an organization, they will bubble all the way up to the top of the organization. Why? Because as people are promoted up the line, they carry the culture with them. As with Allen, the way he saw it done is the way he learned to do it. And it is the way he will continue to do it. This is the meaning of tradition and the powerful role it plays in perpetuating a company's culture.

And let's not forget

Where there are excuses, there will be projection of blame, entitlement attitudes, reactive thinking, can't do attitudes, poor teamwork, pessimism, non-risk-taking, incompetence, disrespect, avoidance of issues, lack of focus, helplessness, self-deceit, procrastination, non-results orientation, lack of creativity, absence of stretching to keep commitments, distrust, conflictual relationships, fear of failure, nonaccountability, denial of responsibility, follower mentality, victimization mindsets, short-term focus, and much, much more. *These are the viruses that are sapping the energy—and the vitality—from corporate American. The good news is that they will all die off when we eliminate excuses from the workplace.*

The Point

Those in leadership positions determine what the corporate culture will be. When companies have a negative culture (i.e., an excuse-making culture) and those at the top are moving in the same direction due to tradition, you have companies that are, or soon will be, in trouble in today's economy. On the other hand, when companies have a negative culture and the leaders are moving in the direction of an excuse-free culture, you have companies hard at work, well-focused, and destined to achieve the winning edge in the marketplace.

Again, the only way to achieve the latter of these two alternatives is to start by recognizing that leadership and management/administration are very different concepts. Does it make sense to assume that an outstanding defensive end in professional football would be an effective head coach for some football franchise? Defensive ends and head coaches are quite different beings. Not that one can't become the other in some instances, just as some good managers become effective leaders in corporations. But to assume that being effective in one position makes you unquestionably effective in another is simply invalid.

The point is, *to assume either that good managers are automatically promotable to leadership positions, or to assume that good managers and administrators are the leaders in your company, is to unknowingly participate in an excuse-making corporate culture, the cost of which in dollars is astronomical.* Effective leadership—the type that will provide the impetus to lead your company into the winner's circle by creating an excuse-free organization—does not happen through allowing the wheels of tradition to grind on and on. Effective leaders must be sought out, hired, promoted, rewarded, developed, and trained. This is no small task. But it is certainly possible once the problem is recognized.

How do you recognize a true leader according to our specific definition of leadership?

I. First and Foremost, a Leader Has Vision

Vision is a guiding purpose that propels a leader forward. He knows where he wants to go; he thinks futuristically; he looks forward. His vision serves as a beacon, and nothing will deter him from the accomplishment of that vision. There is no room for excuses in a leader's primary purpose. Excuses will only get in his way. He simply doesn't have time for them. Jimmy Johnson, the former head coach of the Dallas Cowboys and Miami Dolphins who guided Dallas to two consecutive Super Bowl victories, had a vision of winning the Super Bowl when he took over the reins of a failing football organization. His first year he won very few games. But he was never deterred from his vision. Despite his many differences with owner Jerry Jones, the same one that led to his eventual departure, he refused to let those differences interfere with where he was going. They never became an excuse for not realizing his vision.

2. A Leader Has Respect for Authority

This surprises most people because we tend to think that leaders *are* the authority and that they don't need to have respect for it outside of themselves. But whether a leader's authority figure is a supervisor, a customer, a checkbook, or even God, you must have respect for an outside authority, whoever or whatever it is. Let's look at an example of one outside authority that you always have in business, namely your customers. If you're not respectful of their authority, you soon begin to lose them. And if you lose too many, you're out of business. Suppose an important customer isn't receiving delivery of a critical product when he needs it. Do you call that customer and give him the excuse, "I'm sorry, but my production people haven't been doing their job lately," or do you respect the authority of that customer and figure out how to get him what he needs, regardless? *It is not possible to respect authority and make excuses.* The two just don't go together. There is a job to get done, and excuses cannot be allowed to get in the way. It is people who don't respect authority who give excuses. They are busy projecting the blame elsewhere.

3. A Leader Is Self-Confident

People who are self-confident don't make excuses—not because they never fail, but because they are willing to admit to their own mistakes. Those with a high level of self-confidence will not be afraid to follow their guiding vision. They see failure as a valuable learning experience, not as the end of the road. Self-confidence is something that is pervasive. It relates closely to self-esteem. The leader who isn't self-confident and doesn't feel good about himself won't be given the opportunity to lead for very long. People who would otherwise follow soon sense the leader's lack of self-confidence, and they abandon that person to gravitate to some other individual who is self-confident—someone to whom they can attach themselves.

4. A Leader Is Enthusiastic

Enthusiasm, self-confidence, high self-esteem, and optimism are all closely related concepts. The enthusiastic leader is someone whom people look forward to being around. He is someone who will maintain an even keel in an organization and not allow moods to get low. He can sense it when people are having down moments, and his enthusiasm will help pick them up. Enthusiasm is infectious, and those who have it are those whom others return to for a boost to their batteries when the going gets tough. Enthusiasm attracts people, and this is what makes those who have it such effective leaders. People with enthusiasm are people who generally take responsibility, don't project blame, and don't have time for excuses. They are proactive people who are typically on the move toward achievement of their goals. They have things to do, places to go to, and people to see. Their rule is "let's get it done" rather than "let's make excuses."

5. A Leader Has a High Energy Level

Energy is a direct descendent of the optimism of people who are looking forward. Leaders cannot be looking backwards. They must be continually focusing on their objective, and this requires—and generates—high levels of energy. Energy is not just the speed at which people work, but also the length to which people work. Many individuals want to get ahead in life, but too often they don't want to do what is necessary to make that happen. Success requires long, hard hours. It takes a high energy level to maintain this activity. There have been numerous studies that have linked physical fitness to success in the workplace. There is a direct correlation between physical fitness, high energy, and success. Energetic people have the ability to go into afterburn. Good leaders are people who, when they find themselves in very difficult situations, without much time to act, can call on their energy, fire the afterburners, and go into the hyperdrive speed that allows them to do whatever has to be done in a limited period of time.

6. Leaders Focus on the Big Picture

The difference between vision and focusing on the big picture involves the issue of not being sidetracked. Many people have vision, but they aren't effective leaders because they lose sight of the big picture and let the small issues distract them. Once a true leader is focused on the bigger picture, he's not going to be sidetracked or daunted by small failures or problems along the way. He realizes that it is acceptable, sometimes even necessary, to lose some battles in order to win the war. Therefore, the leader will take the smaller setbacks in stride, and he will have no compelling need to rationalize, project blame, externalize, or make excuses.

7. A Leader Is an Intuitive and Inductive Decision-Maker

He surrounds himself with a wealth of information from which to make his decisions. He trusts his intuitive powers to help lead him in the right direction. And he has developed a decision-making process that allows him to see trends and make accurate predictions based on particular facts. An intuitive and inductive decision-maker is proactive rather than reactive, and therefore has little need or room for excuses, either from himself or others.

8. Leaders Expect Success

Good leaders create an expectation of success in whatever they undertake. They expect it from themselves, and they expect it from those whom they lead. If you expect success from others, then by definition you will not accept excuses. The expectation of success propels you through all the diversions. It is the antithesis of excuse-making. It is no option behavior. Don Shula, former head coach of the Miami Dolphins, always expected his players to play penalty-free games. As a result, the Dolphins led the league year after year in fewest penalties.

Leaders don't expect to fail, so they "backstop" themselves for failures along the way. The concept of backstopping involves the recognition that, like all human beings, the leader has certain weaknesses and shortcomings that need to be compensated for in the people around him. The leader must leverage his strengths, and hire toward his weaknesses. That in itself is the direct opposite of excuse- making. The leader expects to succeed, so he does not allow cracks in which excuses can grow.

9. Leaders Are Self-Disciplined

No matter what the job, no matter what the task, there will always be elements that are distasteful The ability to have the self-discipline to do the unpleasant means that you are going to accept responsibility for the end result. People who don't have self-discipline will always be able to find an excuse for not doing the difficult, unpleasant, and distasteful things.

10. Leaders Are Willing to Take Risks

You can't risk unless you are willing to fail (even though you expect to succeed). You're not willing to fail unless you have the self-confidence to face that failure. You can't face failure unless you are willing to take responsibility for your actions, and you're not going to take responsibility for your actions if you project blame by making excuses. Good leaders will take risks, and they will have managers and administrators around them to serve as checks and balances to help mitigate any loss from dangerously high risks.

In addition, effective leaders will take the risk of allowing others around to experience failure. When the leader is focused on the big picture, he sees that a few small failures by those whom he leads are of little significance. Yet the lessons learned from those failures can make a huge difference in the development of his people. A true leader understands the distinction between "failing to learn" and "failing, to learn."

11. A Leader Has Mental Toughness and Emotional Stability

This entails a wide range of things. but basically what it says is that a person has himself or herself together and does not feel easily frightened or threatened by situations or personalities. If you have emotional and mental strength, you are willing to face your shortcomings and your weaknesses, try to understand them, and do what is necessary to overcome them. You are also willing to confront issues, including criticism that others may make of you. You are willing to hear the bad news. Mentally tough and emotionally stable people do not need to rely on excuses. They can look at things the way they really are. This characteristic is essential for leaders because they must lead through the waters of "what really is," not what he or others unrealistically hope or wish things to be. In other words, leaders have the mental toughness and emotional stability to be grounded in the reality of the situation, whatever that situation is.

12. Leader Will Recognize the Need for Additional Knowledge

Effective leaders never profess to know it all. They realize there is always more to learn and there are different ways of doing things. They are willing to submit themselves to the stresses and strains of a mentor relationship. They are willing to admit that they don't always know what to do. People who are willing to accept the fact that they need to learn more are also willing to admit to failures and inadequacies, and to subject themselves to discomfort in trying something new and different. And this is not the sign of someone who is an excuse-giver. Quite the opposite is true.

13. A Leader Is a Good listener

There is a very ironic twist here. Most people perceived as leaders are those who are giving inspiring advice in their attempts to lead people to greater things. But let's face it, the best teaching method—and a good leader has to be a good teacher—is through self-discovery. This means encouraging others to use their own minds and develop their own problem-solving skills. A leader can do this by listening to the ideas and opinions of his subordinates. *The first sign of greatness in a leader is the ability to develop greatness in others.* You cannot develop good leadership qualities in others unless you are a good listener.

We've seen many CEO's who think they are good leaders because they are good "tellers." But the problem is, as soon as they are out of the picture, their organization is incapable of effective operation because their people have turned to followers. A leader who leads by telling breeds followers. And breeding followers invites excuses when the followers can't operate without their leader.

14. Leaders Are Lucky

Effective leaders tend to have good luck. Ineffective "leaders" tend to have bad luck. Luck is a funny thing. When Gary Player was at his peak as a professional golfer, someone said to him, "You're a very lucky golfer." He responded, "Yes, the more I practice the luckier I get." Luck is a perception of others more than anything else. Good leaders will admit to luck, while poor leaders tend to take credit for luck. Luck is the result of persistence, observation, the ability to focus on the right thing at the right time, and the absence of excuses. If you do these things, you're going to get lucky and you're going to win. Sometimes you're going to win for reasons that you don't understand at the time, and this is what most people call luck. *Luck is when preparation meets with opportunity, and the opportunity is recognized and seized.* If a person prepares enough, is persistent enough, and refuses to be an excuse-maker, he will get lucky sooner or later.

15. A Leader Is Introspective

Good leaders are those who are willing to look at themselves and face their failures without externalizing and making excuses. Leaders must always be improving, and the way they're going to improve is by examining themselves and admitting their weaknesses and failures. Introspection takes time. It is a discipline that requires from one-half to one hour a day to really perfect. Introspection is vitally important to effective leadership because, in a sense, it continuously hones all of the other leadership qualities.

16. Leaders Have Integrity

Integrity is more of a personal trait than anything else. People with integrity are honest, they are trustworthy, and they do the things that are right regardless of the personal consequences to themselves in many instances. Because of this, people with integrity are consistent in the way they deal with certain circumstances. To help see the importance of integrity in a leader, look at a person without integrity. This person shirks responsibility and avoids admitting to weakness or failure. He will project blame, make excuses, and refuse to accept responsibility. Anyone who has tried to follow the lead of an individual without integrity knows what an impossible task that is.

17. Leaders Have Control

Many people in leadership positions feel as if they are out of control, often even admitting to that fact. The primary reason a leader goes out of control is because he is unable to differentiate between real issues and excuses.

There is one behavior that a leader must be in control of above all others, and that is excuse-making behavior. As soon as a leader accepts excuses, he surrenders control. At that point, the excuse-making disease has taken control over the operation of that leader's company (or his unit in the company).

18. A Leader Is Decisive

People within companies often can't make decisions because those in leadership positions can't, or won't. It has never been more true than in corporate America today that *he who hesitates is lost.* Being decisive wasn't as necessary in the past. Corporations could use their momentum to run over the competitor that challenged them. Today, however, time is of the essence. A company can go from market dominance to collapse in a few years as opposed to a few decades. Never before has it been so important that our leaders be decisive.

19. A Leader Is a Good Communicator

Traditionally, an effective communicator was one who was good at "telling." To communicate meant to inform. The good communicator typically could write or speak clearly, if not eloquently. The leader that is capable of demanding excuse-free behavior, however, places more emphasis on mutual understanding than on his eloquence. His goal is to make sure that those he leads comprehend his vision and understand his expectations. Otherwise, his plan won't work. When people don't understand, they are set up to fail. And when failure is imminent, so is excuse-making.

20. A Leader Is Sensitive

To what? To other people's feelings. A leader must not embarrass or humiliate those whom he leads. People tend to become self-protective—even to the point of being dishonest—if they are not treated with dignity and respect. The effective leader assumes the self-worth of others, and works to build trust with them. Only in this context will it be safe for employees to not give excuses when faced with threatening situations.

The Point, Once Again

Leadership and management/administration are, by definition, different concepts. When leadership is understood in a company as the same thing as management and administration, or when those in positions of leadership have been promoted from the ranks of managers and administrators, *the "leaders" will likely not be prepared to lead the company into an excuse-free culture unless they have been properly trained to do so.* And such training is rare.

Remember. if you want to change the culture of an organization, you must begin with the leaders. It is their responsibility to bring about the desired changes. But to effectively change the culture, your leaders must be *true* leaders. That means that the majority of the criteria just discussed must be met, or the results will be—whether you like to think so or not—an excuse-ridden culture.

Essentially, to ensure that you have the leaders who can make your culture excuse-free, you have one of two choices. Either you train the people you currently have according to the accurate definition of what constitutes an effective leader, or you move the current people out and hire new leaders who possess the appropriate qualities. It's that simple.

In Review

- **A corporation that is burdened with excuses is less than a fully functioning company. Megadollars are being lost that could otherwise be made.**

- **An excuse-ridden culture can only be changed with the proper leadership.**

- **The first step toward making that change is to recognize that the problem is both spawned and perpetuated through confused perceptions of what leadership is.**

- **One of the major reasons that our corporations have become excuse-infested is because the source of the problem is built into the very heart of the corporate system. This is why until now it has gone mostly unrecognized. That problem is the promotion of people into leadership positions who have been trained to think like managers** and administrators. This statement is not intended as an attack on managers and administrators. Far from it. *Effective managers and administrators are indispensable to the successful operation of a company. It's just that they may not be as effective at managing change (i.e., leading) as your culture requires.* Managing change demands different skills, different beliefs, different goals, different traits. Managing policy and managing change are as different as night and day.

· *The elimination of excuses from the workplace begins and ends in leadership.* There are only two options. Either train those who are currently in leadership positions to be leaders, or replace them with people who have strong leadership qualities. There are no other choices if you want your company devoid of reactive thinking, can't do attitudes, poor teamwork, conflictual relationships, short- term focus, denial of responsibility, projection of blame, and so on. When leaders target the elimination of excuses, all these other corporate poisons are flushed out. When this is accomplished, results will certainly happen. And your company will be well on its way to recapturing first place.

CHAPTER 9

In Planning

Two of the biggest problems in corporate America today are *lack of focus and lack of consistency.* Goal-setting and planning are intended to prevent these problems. The fact that many companies still struggle with these issues suggests that the entire planning process is often fraught with excuses.

That being the case, it is important to explore some of the reasons why and how this is true. If we can grasp the dynamics of how excuses manifest themselves in the corporate planning process, we will have taken a giant stride toward seeing the immensity, the subtlety, and the destructive potential of the problem of excuses in the workplace. Not the least of these is the fact that excuses cost our companies literally billions of dollars every year.

Definition

Plan, n, An outline; a draft; a map. A scheme for making, doing, or arranging something; a project; a program; a schedule.

Plan, v. *The act of developing* an outline, draft, map. The act of developing a scheme for making, doing, or arranging something, etc.

The Problem of Confusing the Two

We invite you to take a long, hard look at the fact that the word "plan" is both a noun and a verb. That may seem insignificant at first, but in the corporate world it is anything but insignificant. The confusion by leadership between the noun and verb meanings of the word "plan" leads to difficulties of far-reaching proportions in the workplace. "Plan" as a noun is a thing, a document, a product, a blueprint, a map. "Plan" as a verb is a process, an action.

If you ask company owners, presidents, and CEO's the question "Is planning important?" The majority would answer that it is. Yet what "the planning process" means to most of them is that they must somehow end up with a written document that they can thereafter refer to as "the plan: This is exactly what "plan" means in the noun sense of the word. Consequently, most companies have one or more of the following:

- **a strategic plan**
- **a business plan**
- **a sales and marketing plan**
- **an operations plan**
- **a product development plan**

In many cases, large sums of money have been invested to develop such plans. Yet most of them are not living, breathing entities. Odds are that they are sitting on a bookshelf collecting dust or are neatly filed away in some obscure drawer or cabinet, out of sight and all but forgotten.

Why Does This Happen?

As a general rule, smaller companies create plans because of some external influence. For example, the SBA, the bank, or the shareholders may require it. If it's not an external factor that is requiring it, it is an outside source that is influencing it. Or the CEO may read a book that inspires a desire to generate a plan, or he may overhear other CEO's talking about their business plans. As a result, unfortunately, the vast majority of plans are driven by external pressure to prepare them.

It may well be the case that an outside source, such as the bank, may want planning to occur as a *process,* as in the verb sense of the word. The problem is that when those who prepare the plans are only fulfilling a requirement from the outside, they place relatively little value on it. The result is that the plan becomes a product (noun) rather than a process (verb) The purpose of the plan in the preparers' minds may be simply to impress those who will be reading it. As a result we have a multitude of independent consultants who specialize in putting together business plans for companies, or in helping companies put together business plans for themselves. Since business plans are sometimes judged on the basis of volume and appearance, the resulting plans are too often little more than window dressing.

Now this is not an inexpensive process. Companies can spend many thousands of dollars to get such a plan done. But even more importantly, the plan will have very little value to the company beyond satisfying the needs or requirements of the outside source. There is no attempt to systematically communicate the plan throughout the ranks, there is no buy-in by the employees of the company, and there is no way to measure progress or regress with regard to achieving the goals as set forth in the plan. So what happens to it? On the shelf it goes, thus making the whole project a waste of time and money. This is a perfect example of what we mean by "plan" in the noun sense of the word.

In Bigger Companies

In mid-sized and larger companies, planning might be done for some of the same reasons—for example, to meet the expectations of the board of directors. An additional motivation in bigger companies, however, is that planning is one of those things that corporations are just supposed to do.

Imagine for a moment that we pay a visit to The Average Corporation, USA. We seek out all the executives, managers, and administrators. Then we ask each of them separately (and confidentially so it doesn't upset the boss) the following question: "What do you think of the planning process around here?" Most of them would probably admit that they see very little value in it.

Why? Because the plan was prepared for the wrong reasons—to create a product that ends up on the shelf. Since it is not perceived as having any real value, efforts to revive the plan will not be taken seriously, and the plan (noun) becomes even less valuable. While those asked might agree that coming up with a plan is an important thing to do (because the boss tells them it must be done), they also see it as a time waster and as a distraction from their daily work routines. They will generally look at it as something that the boss handed down to them, but that is going to have little if any consequence to the company.

Subsequently, for the majority of people the whole planning process becomes an exercise in futility. Sure, the plan will be prepared as required, and it will probably look good. People will generally put their most optimistic projections into the plan to put the best face on it. But when it's all finished, chances are that it will be set aside to collect dust, right beside the plans from last year and the year before that and the years before that. And it will more than likely never be reviewed again, not even at year's end—which further magnifies the feelings of futility among all who had a hand in preparing it.

What Does This Have To Do with Excuses?

Whether a company approaches the "plan" as a product or as an active process is a function of the culture of that company. _The "plan" is nothing more nor less than_ *the solidification and the manifestation of the corporate culture.* If the culture is reactive, we will find the plan sitting on the shelf—except when it is dusted off for the purpose of finding out who to blame. If the culture is pessimistic, or tolerates procrastination and irresponsibility, or is short-term focused, or exhibits poor teamwork, or demonstrates can't-do attitudes, we will find the plan sitting on the shelf. And if you find a company plan sitting on the shelf, you will also find an abundance of can't-do attitudes, short-term focus, procrastination, denial of responsibility, and so on in that company. Count on it! They always go together.

In short, *wherever there are strategic plans, business plans, sales and marketing plans,* **any kind of plans** *that are collecting dust or filling drawer space, there you have an excuse-making culture.* And because that is true, you also have all of the members of the family that go with excuses living in your corporate environment, whether or not they are welcome, and whether or not you like it. That's just the way it is because of the systemic nature of the problem.

Corporations Tend to Encourage Excuses

Earlier in this book we pointed out the tendency of corporations to allow and even indirectly encourage excuses. Nowhere is this more true than in the planning process. Let's look more closely at how this phenomenon happens.

Corporation XYZ goes through a yearly planning process. Bill, the CEO, mandates that the process is to begin on November 1 and must be concluded by December 21 in order to get it out to all the employees by the beginning of the January-through-December fiscal year. This same planning procedure has happened for several years at XYZ. So Bill's only real job is to remind the management staff in October that the date is soon approaching and to get ready to go through the process. He may do this by copying last year's memo, penciling in the new date, and having his secretary retype it and distribute a copy to each manager.

The planning process itself is built around a departmental questionnaire that was introduced by an outside consulting firm six years ago, for which the company paid a sizeable fee. The manager of each department is expected to collect the information through meetings with his people, build it into a departmental report, and submit it to the CEO's office by December 21.

Here We Go Again!

Every year the planning process happens in approximately the same way. The managers grumble about the extra workload, but of course don't say anything to Bill, since he's the one who mandated it. They postpone tackling the project until the last possible minute, at which time they call a few quick departmental meetings with the people they manage. Most of the people in each of the departments gripe and complain about having to "do this stupid questionnaire one more time," wondering what good it does. Like Bill, they hunt down last year's material and make a few small changes here and there before photocopying it.

In the end, the reports somehow get completed and are submitted to Bill on time. He reads them over, consolidates them, and thereby builds his plan for the upcoming fiscal year.

On December 29 a newsletter from the CEO's office is released to each of the managers, forecasting the market and making projections for the year. Finally, after several narratives, comes the bottom line: "WE EXPECT THE MARKET TO TAKE A SLIGHT TURN DOWNWARD THIS YEAR. WE ALL MUST TIGHTEN OUR BELTS AND FIND WAYS TO CUT COSTS. IF WE DO THAT AND WORK TO MAINTAIN OUR CURRENT LEVEL OF SALES, WE WILL ACTUALLY SHOW PROFIT OF AROUND 10 PERCENT OVER THE NEXT YEAR." The report concludes with a few pages of numbers detailing how much each department can spend, and what the sales numbers will have to be.

Once the managers have received the newsletter from the CEO's office, it now becomes their responsibility to communicate this "plan" to the employees at their first departmental meeting in January. And they do. And everyone hears it. And everyone says, "Fine, okay." And the plan goes on the shelf and stays there, collecting dust.

Now if this example is a bit trite, it is also more than a bit accurate. It represents the way that many, many companies go about the so-called "planning process." It is based on "plan" as a noun. The attitude seems to be, "Let's get a document, a product, that we can circulate throughout the company, and then be done with it."

Now Come the Excuses

Let's jump ahead to October of the same year. Nine of the ten departments have overspent their budgets. Bill confronts the managers of each of these departments and asks what happened. This is what he hears.

- **"I told my people. They just don't listen." (Denial of responsibility. projection of blame. Victimization, externalization.)**

- **"Costs have gone up over what was projected. We could only cut out so much and still function." (Denial of responsibility. projection of blame. Victimization, externalization.)**

- **"It will improve over the next couple of months, promise." (Self-deceit.)**

- **"We did the best we could." (Helplessness.)**

- **"Your projections might have been a little too optimistic." (Denial of responsibility, projection of blame, externalization.)**

- **"A couple of our people were spending way over their budgets. But we got rid of them when we found out what was happening." (Reactive thinking, projection of blame, denial of responsibility, externalization.)**

Do you see what these are? These are all excuses, and, as such, they point to the dangerous conditions in the parentheses, which are the same ones that lie beneath _the waterline in the iceberg. These conditions—denial of responsibility, projection of blame, and so on—seriously jeopardize the overall effectiveness of the corporation._

So What Does This Mean?

When corporations proceed with the planning process as if "plan" were a noun, that process both _expresses_ and _spawns_ an excuse-making culture. Most companies believe that the plan (noun) should forecast what will happen in the coming year. Yet projections in the plan will inevitably be unrealistic because changes will occur during the year—changes in the market, changes in product, changes in personnel, and so on. Because of these changes, it is unlikely that people will be able to live up to all the expectations spelled out in the plan.

Hence employees are "forced" to protect themselves against criticism and blame, and they do this by making excuses. This is what we mean by saying that corporations tend to encourage excuses. There is nothing devious about it on either side. Making excuses is an automatic, spontaneous, instantaneous reaction by individuals—managers and employees alike—to avoid emotional pain, including the criticism of not meeting the expectations as spelled out in the plan (noun).

When Planning Is a Verb

Planning in a proactive, creative, optimistic, can-do, stretching, responsible, long-term-focused company is a verb. It is something that you not only _develop_ proactively, you also _implement_ it proactively. It is an ongoing process from the beginning of the year to the end, and then it begins anew. If a plan isn't a working plan, it is no different from an architect's blueprint that never gets pulled out of its cardboard tube. Or a professional hockey player's playbook that never once gets opened. We don't build skyscrapers or professional athletic teams with noun-type plans. How can we expect to build healthy organizations that way? Blueprints and play books are dog-eared, wrinkled, soiled, and spotted with coffee stains and chewing gum. They are used—frequently, if not daily. They are living, breathing documents that reflect the pulse of those whom they serve. This is what a "plan" must be if we are to rid our companies of the fatal disease of excuse-making.

And it can be done!

Planning and Goals

It is not uncommon for corporations to think of "planning" and "goal-setting" as two separate entities. This is because of our tendency to look at "plan" as a noun, as a product, as something to create and then forget about.

Now along comes the task of motivating people. One way to do that is to have them set goals. So time-management seminars and goal-setting workshops are conducted to help people reach for something higher. But they don't work—and they won't work, because these strategies are not integrated into the larger "plan," The notes and other materials from such programs, therefore, just become something more for people to put on the shelf, thereafter to collect dust.

The point is that goal-setting is a meaningless concept unless it is married to the planning process. A viable plan must begin with input from all those affected by the plan. It must proceed with buy-in by everyone and sign-on to the program. Next comes the process of interpreting company goals into departmental goals, again with input from all affected, and buy-in by everyone into the plan. Then comes the interpretation of the departmental goals into individual goals which each employee negotiates with his or her supervisor Finally, the goals must be benchmarked, monitored, measured, upgraded, and adjusted, until they are living, workable periodic goals. Then and only then do you have a "plan" in the healthy, excuse-free sense of the word.

Imagine for a moment what can happen in a company when the business plan is translated into every employee's individual work-related goals, where everyone is responsible for and accountable to those goals, and the progress toward achieving them would be continuously measured and rewarded. What would happen to employee morale? What would happen regarding motivation, incentive, and productivity? Ultimately, what would happen to the bottom line? Clearly, this would be a workplace where there is no room for excuses. Where there is no room for excuses, there is no room for all of its negative cousins, either, and subsequently, *there will be results!*

Planning and Implementation

Often the problem with implementing the corporate plan is not due to the plan itself. Many plans are well conceived and well thought out, often under the guidance of a consulting that specializes in corporate planning. The problem, rather, is in the absence of a plan to implement the plan. Without such a "metaplan," no one is given ultimate responsibility to see it through. The result, of course, will be more excuses. Since there is no accountability for the implementation of the plan, before long it will take a back seat to one crisis or another, and will soon be forgotten. The point is that there must be no excuse for making excuses about not implementing the plan, even if that means revising the plan. Never should a company follow a plan (noun) to its own grave. Rather, it must be committed to the planning process (verb), and that ongoing process might well include changing the plan as needed.

Planning Is a Team Process

A plan—like a chain—is only as strong as its weakest link. Too often we have plans that fall apart because just one individual failed to provide his necessary "link." By definition, a plan is something that is all-encompassing. It brings together multitudes of departments, disciplines, and types of people. But while the planning process is usually a team process, the execution of the plan is too often assumed to be an individual process. One of the breakdowns of plan implementation is that individuals who are left to execute the plans are not held accountable to the team that helped make those plans. This opens the door to all kinds of excuse-making when the plan eventually fails.

Long-Term vs. Short-Term Plans

The planning process consists of two broad categories: long-term and short-term. One of the difficulties companies run into is the incongruity between short-term and long-term plans. This relates back to the discussion in Chapter 7 about corporate culture. In an excuse-laden culture, short-term thinking is prevalent. Short-term is where the crises are, and crises always capture immediate attention. This makes long-term planning almost impossible. Furthermore, if any long-term planning does occur, it will typically be at odds with the short-term focus that results from reacting to one crisis after another.

A Diagnostic Tool

One clear indicator of an excuse-laden company is that virtually everything has top priority. Everything is a crisis. It is a mentality of constantly fighting brush fires. There is no primary direction and purpose, so it's impossible to set priorities. A company that doesn't set priorities is a company that's not planning effectively. And a company that's not planning effectively is a company full of excuses.

Where Should Plans Start?

There has been a good deal of debate lately as to whether plans should start at the top of an organization and negotiate their way down, or whether they should start at the bottom and accumulate as they go up until they become a master plan. The truth is that it probably doesn't make any difference where the planning begins. What *does* make the difference is whether or not there is buy-in and ownership (acceptance of responsibility for one's own part) at all levels. If you don't have ownership, excuse-making will naturally happen.

Here is an example we see time and again. Corporate headquarters will set a budget. Nobody in the various divisions will say anything as to whether the plan is good or bad, achievable or not achievable. They just shrug their shoulders, and then halfway into the fiscal year they say things like, "We're never going to make that budget." "They don't know what it's like in the field." "They don't understand that we can't get our workers to produce at that level for the amount of money we're allowed to pay them." "It wasn't realistic in the first place." "We didn't set it.

In fact, they never even consulted with us." "We don't have to worry about it. We don't even have to take responsibility for it."

What is this except one excuse after another? Ownership is a big chunk of what it takes to get rid of excuses. If you have ownership of a plan, you have the basis for being able to take excuses out of performance.

Measurement and Adjustment

Another reason why the planning process can fail miserably is because of the lack of measurement to evaluate whether or not the plan is being achieved. Periodic measurement helps to keep "plan" as a verb. People, if left to their own devices, don't like to have a plan. They are more than happy to let the plan lapse into its noun form. Goals frighten and stretch us, and move us out of our comfort zones. Goals keep people from doing things the way they've always done them in the past.

The point is that the loftiest of plans and the best of goals will die on the vine unless there is accountability to the plan through measuring the progress and adjusting behaviors as necessary along the way.

"Plan" As a Verb Is All-Encompassing

In order for "plan" to be a verb rather than a noun, planning must (1) penetrate vertically throughout the organization, and (2) include things that are usually not thought of as part of the planning process: personal planning, written goals, agendas for meetings, interest in what will happen in the future of the company as it relates to one's job, and so on. Without these, planning cannot be a living, breathing function of the organization. And where it is not a living, breathing function of the organization, there will not be results, but there will be plenty of excuses.

In Conclusion

- "Plan" as a verb always has value even if the goals are not always reached. Much of the value of planning is in the process, during which everyone in the company takes an active, responsible role. The planning process is as important, if not more important, than the final written plan.

- "Plan" as a noun has value only if it is the result of a carefully designed planning process. In terms of results, perfect execution of an ill-conceived plan looks much like poor execution of a well-conceived plan. It is important to make sure that your plan is properly prepared, because therein lies your only hope for proper execution. Otherwise your people are set up to fail, and they will be "forced" to protect themselves with excuses and where there are excuses, there will be a multitude of other corporate sins. Plan on it.

Notes and Quotes

We have forty million reasons for failure, but not single excuse.

Rudyard Kipling

CHAPTER 10

In Teamwork

Teamwork in organizations was a relatively obscure concept a few years back. Today, everybody in corporate America is talking about it. Why the big emphasis on work teams in recent years?

Definition

Teamwork, n. 1. Joint action by a group of people, in which each person subordinates his or her individual interests and opinions to the unity and efficiency of the group; coordinated effort, as of an athletic team. 2. Work done by or with a team.

Why Have Teams?

The trend for corporations in today's economy is to downsize. As of the writing of this book, about 3,000 people per day are being let go from their jobs in this country. This downsizing trend is designed to cut the fat from organizations, to go "flatter," as they say. This flattening effort is aimed particularly at cutting out layers of middle management so there are fewer people between the top layers and the bottom layers of a company, thus "flattening out" the organization.

In the past, it was not uncommon for the typical manager to manage from two to five employees. Now, because of downsizing and flattening, the typical manager is managing between 20 and 40 employees. Because of this, there is less opportunity for managers to interact with, supervise, and direct their people. This is the first reason why teamwork has become so important in our companies. It is a way to compensate for the direction that was previously furnished by management.

The Age of Specialization

A second factor that has required better use of the team concept is the movement in our society away from generalists and toward specialists. As a result of this trend, very few people know a lot about many different things. Instead, most people know a lot about some specific thing.

So in order to accomplish a specific goal or task, it is often necessary to employ the talents of numerous people in some type of team setting. If you look at the average company today, the level of expertise within the company has increased tremendously over the past few years. The technical skills required and the technical abilities available have dramatically increased. This means that each player generally brings more to the table now than in the past. There is more innovation today than at any other time in history. These new ideas are coming less often from CEO's and more often from work team members.

Effective Teamwork vs. Ineffective Teamwork

It is fairly easy to recognize good teamwork: the result is that the job gets done. Through cooperative and coordinated effort, a good work team is notably productive and efficient. A group that works well together is indeed a thing of beauty.

What's maddening in the corporate structure are those situations when the job doesn't get done through teamwork, and the results are not there. While it is easy to recognize an ineffective work team, it is *very* difficult to recognize the cause of the ineffectiveness. Poor teamwork can be the manifestation of several possible problems.

Why Teamwork Fails

1. Bad work teams will generally do such a good job of externalizing and excuse-making that it is almost impossible to see the real problem. Furthermore, the whole team can come to a consensus on an excuse. (This is not devious, remember—it is an unconscious function, in this case, of the group.) Therefore excuses tend to be accepted even more as "explanations" or "reasons" by the sheer force of numbers. So when a team gives an excuse, it naturally has more validity than when an individual gives an excuse.

2. There may not have been a clearly defined, understood, and *accepted* set of accountabilities for each member of the team. This is sometimes due to a lack of clarity about what exactly the entire team is supposed to accomplish. But more often, it is due to ambiguity in the determination of individual responsibilities: Who is supposed to do what, how, by when, etc. When the specifics are not clearly spelled out, most teams will weaken. When the team members report back for progress, something important will have been left out, or will have fallen through the cracks. Again, this is because the particular task wasn't originally conceptualized as part of the charter, or it wasn't clearly understood which team member (or members) were responsible for it.

3. As team members jockey for power (as people tend to do), they will sometimes overcommit and accept too much responsibility, or accept responsibility for something they aren't qualified to do. A team situation sometimes creates a level of enthusiasm in the group that is difficult for any one individual to maintain apart from the group. It is the tendency for any group to take on, shall we say, a temporary "personality" of its own. This temporary personality will fade as the enthusiasm of the group fades. When this happens, the result will be failure in one form or another. And where there is failure, there will also be externalization of the problem, projection of blame, and more excuses than you can shake a stick at.

4. Teamwork implies working among your peers. Peers are less likely to hold each other accountable than managers are. There is a certain insecurity in trying to hold a peer accountable. It tends to bring up all the old, negative messages from childhood about being a tattletale. Yet by not holding a peer accountable within a group, you help disguise the real issues. That is, you allow for excuse-making.

5. It is not uncommon for a team to have one person who tries to dominate, control, gain power over, or in some other way negatively influence the group. Sometimes you can see that this is a person who is utilizing the team to gain his own power base. Whether his motivation is low self-esteem, lack of self-confidence, revenge against someone in management, or some other reason, such a player may cause a team to fail. The other team members may resent such behavior and begin to work at cross purposes. Some team members may even intentionally sabotage the team's effort and cause it to fail so that the power-hungry person would look bad. This type of scenario is a real hotbed for excuses, since no one will give the real reason for the lack of results.

6. One of the inherent problems with the teamwork concept is that, by usual standards, it requires players who fit the middle of the spectrum. That's what a team player is expected to be. The individuals on the extremes are generally not good team players. Yet often it's the people on the extremes who have the most to offer. The best teams are not made up of clones, but of a diversity of people. Yet when someone selects a team, he generally picks people with whom he's comfortable and who are similar to him in many ways. By so doing, the differences, the extremes, will be overlooked, and this could have a devastating effect on the total team effort. Since the team concept is important for the future of our corporations, we need to find ways to include those people on the extremes and make them a functional part of the team process. We must stop finding excuses for leaving out of the teamwork effort some of our most valuable resources.

The Point

Teamwork is a concept that is easily misunderstood, so it's possible to approach the whole subject from the wrong direction. A popular belief is that if your team isn't working well together, it helps to put the players in some type of experience where they must depend on each other for their safety. Weekend trust walks, ropes courses, climbing exercises, and similar programs are famous for this. The strategy may be, for example, to put the team in a dangerous situation where they have to depend on each other to keep from getting hurt.

These experiences tend to create an adrenaline rush that leaves everybody feeling good about what happened. But they are unreal—not grounded in the real problems of everyday life. So on Monday morning these same team members find themselves back at work facing the identical problems that they left behind on Friday. And, all too often, the team handles those problems in exactly the same way as before. Why? Because such team exercises rarely address the *real* reasons—the six just discussed—why teamwork doesn't work. Until those reasons are properly addressed, any team, because of the very nature of the team concept, is at risk of failing on a regular basis.

A Point to Remember

It merits a moment's review to say again what happens when people face the possibility of failure. To protect themselves from embarrassment, criticism, blame, or emotional hurt in any form, people will automatically, unknowingly, and yet very creatively *make excuses*. This behavior is a self-protective mechanism that is born into us. It is part of being human.

Therefore

When a team is failing up, or has failed, no one is likely to step forward and take full responsibility. Instead, each of the team members will probably be called in individually by their managers, free to make their own excuses *apart from the team* as to why the effort failed. And you can be sure that the excuses will take the form of blame projected onto someone or something else.

That this happens is one of the factors that allows for, if not encourages, the breakdown of the team effort. This closed-door posturing with management is likely to evoke excuses and finger pointing by each of the players, which in turn creates animosity among the other team members. The greater the animosity, the more likely other members are to give additional excuses to protect themselves, and the problem snowballs. The result is that everyone involved (management included) gets steered off course, and the real problem ends up not getting fixed at all—or at best the solution is greatly delayed.

In Conclusion

Many of our traditional views of teamwork create a context in which people in the workplace make excuses. Excuses are systemic in nature, remember. They "go with" certain other conditions (insufficient accountabilities, procrastination, pessimism, etc.), and they will occur whenever any (or all) of these conditions prevail. *One of the secrets to getting results instead of excuses is to eliminate the conditions in which people are allowed and/or encouraged to make excuses.* We will be giving considerable attention to this principle in Part III.

Suffice it to say here that teamwork is important, and it is necessary. It will no doubt be on the corporate scene for many years to come. But until we come to grips with the real issues that are involved in the team process, we are likely to continue to have high rates of failure from team efforts, along with an abundance of excuses, rather than high-level results.

CHAPTER 11

In Bureaucracies

Like cancer in the human body, excuses are such an insidiously destructive force in our corporate bodies that we must seize every opportunity to identify them, expose them, and systematically destroy them. In this chapter we will provide an opportunity to look at how excuses manifest themselves in bureaucracies. Since most corporations are, by definition, bureaucratic in nature, we think this information will help you identify excuses in your company. Like it or not, what you're about to discover is that bureaucracies are to excuses what swamps are to mosquitoes: they provide a fertile environment in which to multiply. And multiply they do!

Definition

Bu-reauc-ra-cy, n. Administration of an organization through departments and subdivisions managed by sets of officials following a typically inflexible routine.

Their Source

Where do bureaucracies come from? Probably very few people, if any, have ever intentionally set out to create a so-called bureaucracy, yet they exist in abundance. Most people in the corporate world are caught smack in the center of them, yet not everyone recognizes that fact. It's like not being able to see the forest because of all the trees: bureaucracies are so close to us that we can't see them clearly. They are us, which is a big part of the problem. So now did we get in the middle of this bureaucratic mess? Why do bureaucracies have to be a part of the workplace at all?

The Life Cycle of a Business

After working for twelve years at an odd assortment of jobs, Ed decided to start his own industrial detergent business in the basement of his home. That was over thirty years ago. Like so many individuals who venture into the business world on their own, Ed did virtually everything himself in the beginning. He emptied the wastebaskets, did the accounting, handled all the marketing and selling, answered the phone, and serviced his customers. On top of all that, he alone was responsible for the production. At the time, Ed was totally in tune with his customers' needs and wishes. He was, as Barbara Walters on the television series "20/20" is fond of saying. "in touch." He knew everything that was going on in relation to his business, and there was never any question as to whether or not he was responsive to the market's needs. He could respond quickly to any situation because he was a one-man show.

Ed's business began to flourish. As be became more and more successful, his workload became overwhelming. There was much more to do than one person could possibly do well. So Ed made two important business decisions: it was time to move into a larger facility and it was necessary to hire a few people to help him run his business.

The Policy Manual

It wasn't long before Ed came to realize something that most entreprenuers discover when they take on their first employees: the people he hired had a difficult time thinking as he did. Ed soon figured out that be needed to give some attention to managing his help. So be wrote a policy manual. As Ed knew when he wrote his first one, a policy manual is a book of company rules and regulations. What he wasn't cognizant of, however, was that same manual was also the first stage of an emerging bureaucracy in his company.

As time passed, Ed's company continued to grow. There were more orders for industrial detergents than he and his employees could manufacture and deliver. So he hired more people. Before long, Ed realized that he was unable to manage all of his people by himself. So he singled out some of his more conscientious employees and promoted them to the ranks of management. It would be their job to enforce the policy manual in each of their respective departments. He assigned one manager to over see sales and marketing, one in manufacturing, one in finance, and one in the office. In terms of reducing the stress on Ed, it proved to be a wise decision. But again, Ed did not see the subtle shift in priorities that was taking place right in his own company. He did not realize the focus was gradually moving from, "Are we responding to the marketplace?" to "Are we following company policy?" Though Ed did not know it at the time, his company was becoming a bureaucracy.

The Conflicts

As the bureaucracy swelled within his company, Ed became increasingly detached from the realities that were going on in the market. He found himself handling conflicts and grievances that resulted from people not following company regulations. Slowly, quietly, invisibly, yet surely, the bureaucracy was growing. Ed was now becoming an enforcer of rules as opposed to a creator of policy designed to respond to the needs of the marketplace.

In the gradual development of Ed's company, there was another distinctive shift occurring. The managers were getting nervous about a phenomenon that often happens in bureaucracies called "kill the messenger syndrome." As you know, in ancient times it was not uncommon for a person who brought bad news to the king or emperor to be put to death. Somehow that was supposed to make the problem go away. In corporate America that same phenomenon gets translated into: if someone up the chain of command doesn't like what he or she hears, get rid of the person who said it!

The point is that the managers who reported to Ed didn't want to be "killed." for bringing the bad news. Bad news could be of two types. It could be something unpleasant about the marketplace, or it could be bad news about policy being broken by employees. Either way, they learned how to hide such things to protect themselves. Consequently, Ed became less involved with the kinds of issues that would lead to increased productivity in the company, and more involved with things that would get in the way of reaching that goal.

And the Bureaucracy Continues to Grow

Jack, one of Ed's original employees. is no longer performing well. Ed doesn't want to hurt Jack, and he doesn't know how to get rid of him. So he moves him into a specially created position. When Ed looks in on Jack four weeks later, he finds that the position is filled not only by Jack, but also by an administrative assistant, a secretary, a file clerk, a copy machine, and a coffee pot. To justify his existence, Jack is usurping the time of other people by creating reports and other paperwork.

And so it is that the bureaucracy continues to grow.

The Dark Days of winter

It is now thirty years since Ed began his business. His company is fraught with problems. Sales are up for three years in a row, but profits are down over the same period because of shrinking margins. The competition has become so keen that the only way the company can survive, and then not for long, is to continue to lower prices.

What has happened to Ed's company over the last thirty years is precisely what has happened with so many big and aging companies in our country. They have lost touch with the marketplace. They have developed so many insulating layers that their entire focus has moved in the direction of ruling themselves rather than fulfilling the needs of their customers.

Herb Kelleher, CEO of Southwest Airlines, realizes the importance of staying in touch with the needs of the customers. He believes that time spent behind his desk is nonproductive time. He purposely tries to gain as much exposure with his customers and employees as possible. Rather than travel on the corporate jet, he flies commercially so as to deal with line personnel, flight attendants, passengers, and so on. It should come as no surprise that Southwest Airlines has the highest profit margin in the business.

The larger organization becomes, the more it tends to accumulate secondary responsibilities to the point that it is unable to focus on its primary responsibilities and purposes. This is because the people who need to be "in the know" often become—by the nature of the system—the ones who are the most removed. Such is the nature of any bureaucracy.

123

A Current Example of the Birth of a Bureaucracy

The amount of information that is now available through the use of technology is absolutely overwhelming. Management teams cannot begin to keep up with it.

Five years ago, Mike ran his business on the basis of five key financial indicators that he monitored weekly. Today he has an entire staff of people who are providing to him 98 key indicators on a weekly basis. Of course, each person thinks his key indicator is the most important. Mike was taxed trying to keep up with five, and now it is absolutely impossible for him to deal with 98. To try to prevent the loss of any gold nuggets in the endless flow of information, he hires more and more administrative assistants to keep track of these 98 indicators. These assistants, by the way, need copy machines and coffee makers, and they must be managed and led.

Now Mike, like most CEO's, is a very busy person. With corporate meetings and all, there are heavy demands on him approximately 70 percent of the time. So only about 30 percent of Mike's time is discretionary. He gets thirty-page monthly reports from his reporting offices, each of which takes an average of 20 hours per month to prepare. When Mike is at his best, he can only analyze and absorb a very small piece of it.

When we think of the compounding effects of all this, what we have here is an executive who is getting a lot of information that he's not using—some of which may be very valuable. And we have a large number of man-hours put into preparing paperwork that is never effectively used by management. We also have a growing staff of people to be managed. What we have, really, is a sprouting bureaucracy, a special type called an "information bureaucracy." This phenomenon is bound to become more common, with many companies not yet realizing that it is already happening to them.

What Does This Have to Do with Excuses?

Everything! First, we've just seen, through the examples of Ed and Mike, how a bureaucracy tends to build layer upon layer of insulation between a company and the marketplace that it serves. What are those layers of insulation really insulating? The unfortunate answer is: reality, truth, *the way it really is* in the world that the bureaucracy was intended to serve. By nature, bureaucracies obscure and water down the truth. Obscured truth is the womb of half-truths, lies, rationalizations, and excuses.

Second, and this may be another way of saying the same thing, remember how Ed's managers disguised the bad news, first to protect Ed, but mainly to protect themselves? If they couldn't tell Ed the whole truth, that means that they felt forced by the system to say something less than the whole truth. Even though Ed's managers would think of themselves as truthful individuals and not liars, nevertheless by the nature of the system—the bureaucracy—they were forced to protect themselves, which they did by making *excuses*.

Which leads us to point number three, perhaps the most important. In any organization, whether public or private, profit or nonprofit, service-or production-oriented, large or small: *when excuses are allowed at the top of an organization* (and this is almost always the case with bureaucracies), *they will be allowed and encouraged throughout that organization.*

Let's say it differently. *Bureaucracies breed excuse-making cultures.* As a general rule. people will make excuses in order to survive at the top levels of a bureaucracy. Yet where there are excuses at the top there is going to be an abundance of excuses throughout the rest of the organization. That's why we've said that bureaucracies are to excuses what swamps are to mosquitoes. Excuses will multiply and infest the entire corporate environment.

In Review

The bad news is that unless there is some strategic intervention, bureaucracies—like lemmings marching to their death at sea—will continue to travel down their self-destructive paths. The evidence is clear. Comparing the lists of the top ten corporations in this country in 1980 and then again in 1990, only

one company made both lists. In the global marketplace, many companies that held top ratings for decades have slipped considerably in the standings.

The good news is that this trend does not have to continue. It is reversible. Some companies have made progress, but they have not yet recaptured the lead in world competition. To do so requires looking through a different lens that makes it possible to see the problem in a new way. Otherwise it's like trying to find a blue line on a piece of paper while looking through a blue lens. It would be nearly impossible to see. That's the way it is with excuses. We haven't seen their destructive potential because we've been looking through an excuse-colored lens. We've been looking through cause/effect and coincidental modalities, and it is impossible to see the enemy from either of those perspectives.

The problem of excuses in the workplace is a massive, systemic problem. Excuses are everywhere. They are almost as common as the air we breathe. Like air, excuse-making is invisible, unless you have the proper instruments with which to spot it. Learning to recognize the problems caused by excuses is like learning to look at three-dimensional art. You can stand in front of the mat and look for quite some time before the hidden picture lifts itself off the screen and comes into clear view. Then, once you've seen it, you wonder how it could have been so difficult to find.

The point is that recognizing that excuses are *indeed* a problem is the first half of the battle. Once that is accomplished, the remedy is not all that far away. Excuse-laden cultures are like alcoholism, which is a disease of denial. For the person with a drinking problem, half the battle is to recognize and admit that he has a problem. So it is with bureaucracies, corpora-tions, cultures, leadership teams, departments, and so on that are infected with excuses. *If we can just see the problem, and admit to it, we can fix it. Until we see it, there is little hope for complete recovery.*

In Part II we have addressed how excuses manifest them-selves in culture, leadership, planning, teamwork, and bureau-cracies. The same infection may be found in customer service, sales departments, production, community relations, and even the boardroom.

Our purpose has been to give you a new perspective on the source of the problem, and to see what happens in companies that have the disease. You cannot know yet to what extent your company is infected, or what to do about the problem. We will tackle that in Part III. To this point, we have wanted you to see more clearly how devastating excuses can be in the corporate set-ting. The problem of excuse-making is systemic-once in the company, it can easily infect the entire corporate body. And whether the corporate body is ailing from excuse-making in whole or in part, either way it is very difficult to achieve winning results. This, again, is because *where there are excuses, there will not be desired results.*

Notes and Quotes

He that is good for making excuses is seldom good for anything else.

Benjamin Franklin

The Solution
to the Problem

How to Eliminate Excuses
from the Workplace

CHAPTER 12

The Commitment Step: To or Not To?

As beneficial as it would be to have no more excuses in your workplace, you may be wondering whether it is really possible to achieve such a state. Perhaps to do so seems like a corporate utopia, rather like trying to achieve a sinless world. You may be asking yourself the question, "How do I know whether or not to move ahead with such a project?"

The purpose of Part III is to help you discover your answer to this question. By the time you finish it, you will have a much clearer understanding of whether or not it is something you want to undertake. In this chapter, we want to discuss some preliminaries to actually getting started.

What Does "Excuse-Free" Really Mean?

We've spoken often of helping you achieve an "excuse-free" organization. However, technically speaking, it may well be impossible to reach this goal because *being totally excuse-free is an ideal state.* As long as there are human beings, there will be excuses, We will likely never totally eradicate this self-protective mechanism from the workplace. But that should not deter us in our efforts to *reach for the goal* of becoming excuse-free in our companies. Olympic gymnastic or diving champions rarely achieve perfect scores, but they never stop striving for perfection in their quest for excellence. *It is the striving for the ideal that makes them number one.*

The effectiveness of ridding your company of excuses might be likened to the Richter scale method of measuring the power of an earthquake, only inversely. An *increase* of 1.0 on the Richter scale multiples the power of the quake by 10; a *decrease* in the number of excuses by 10 multiplies the effectiveness of your company by 10 or perhaps more. The point is, a company doesn't have to be totally excuse-free in order to take giant strides forward in getting results. But it does have to be consciously—and constantly—striving toward the *goal* of becoming excuse-free.

Why?

Let's suppose you start a company from scratch. Intentionally, you make it company policy that excuses are acceptable in your organization, which means that everyone is allowed to deny responsibility, to project blame for their own mistakes, to procrastinate on the accomplishment of tasks, and so on. You would probably agree that this would be a ludicrous and unproductive thing to do, and that the company would have big problems before long.

Yet this is precisely the condition that many of our companies are in today. They are excuse-infested. Not, of course, because excuse-making is part of company policy, but because ridding themselves of excuses is **not** part of company policy. *It is critical to understand that excuse-making is the default position for people if clear corrective measures are not taken by leaders and management.* To default is to "fail to do," and this is exactly what has happened to our organizations, if not our country. It is why we haven't yet recaptured the lead. Excuses are like quack grass or dandelions in our lawns. When we fail to manage their growth, they quickly take over. In much the same way, when we fail to manage excuses, our cultures become excuse-infested.

Said Differently

Excuse-making has generally been ignored in corporate America. People in corporations have simply never before realized its destructive power. Since the management of excuses has never been a line item on the budget, since it's never been evaluated, since it's not information that has ever been gathered from customer surveys, since it's not included on employee evaluation forms, we've just assumed that excuse-making isn't all that important an issue. Failing to recognize that excuses are a problem is what makes them such a big problem.

This must change. And it will only change by effectively managing excuses, which means to consciously—and constantly—strive toward the goal of becoming excuse-free. The closer an organization comes to reaching this ideal, the more effective will be its results, and the further ahead of the competition it will be.

Let's discuss (1) what it takes for a company to be able to change; and then, if those conditions are right, (2) what a company actually has to target for change.

The Necessary Ingredients for Change

Generally speaking, there are three prerequisites that are necessary for any company to make significant, gainful, and lasting change: (1) the leaders must be *ready* to change (2) they must have an intense desire to win; and (3) they must be *willing to make the commitment* to do whatever it takes to become number one in their field. These characteristics are so important that they each deserve a closer look.

Readiness

The first rule of change is that no company changes until its leaders are ready. You may have heard the saying, "When the student is ready to learn, the teacher will appear." By the same token, when the company's leaders are ready to change, the answers will appear. Readiness to change is always a function of discomfort—that is, disliking things the way they are in your company and wanting them to be different. Contentment breeds complacency—and ultimately, defeat by the competition. Discontent breeds initiative, creativity, proactivity, invention, progress, and ultimately, victory. Hence the saying, "Necessity is the mother of invention." Necessity grows from discontent. If you are less than content with the present state of affairs in your company, you may be ready to change.

Desire

You must truly want to lead the competitive race in your market. If you are content with anything less than aiming for first place, then adopting this powerful new formula won't help. It won't help because it won't happen. Though there are rare exceptions to the rule, we all know that champions at *anything* are made, not born. Show us any champion, regardless of his field of endeavor, and we'll show you an individual—or a company full of individuals – with a fierce desire to compete, to excel, and to be number one.

Commitment

There are millions of people in the world, and hundreds of thousands of business owners, who would like their situations to improve. There are far fewer who are committed to doing what it takes to make the changes necessary for improvement.

Genuine commitment (as opposed to lip service) can be measured in four ways:

(1) *the willingness to change* (assuming there is readiness)
(2) *the willingness to risk*
(3) *the willingness to invest time*
(4) *the willingness to invest money.*

Some people like to talk about how committed they are to one thing or another. But if you want to know what someone is *truly* committed to, look at what he does, not at what he says he wants to do. *The commitment to win is evident in action, not intentions.*

What Has to Be Targeted for Change?

Traditionally, companies have placed importance on developing vision statements, mission statements, and, more recently, values statements. Our experience is that these concepts are easy to confuse, since they overlap each other to some degree.

135

But they are also clearly distinct from one another in important ways. You must understand these distinctions in order to know what to target for change.

Before addressing the distinctions, though, we want to make it clear that we are not authorities on vision, mission, and values statements. Much helpful information is available to you on these subjects if you are looking for the opinion of experts. Our only purpose here is to provide working definitions to any reader who may not be familiar with the terms so that you will better understand what comes next.

Vision Statements

A vision statement is a statement about *where* you want your company to be in the future (as compared with where it is now). A vision statement is, in effect, an expression of a long term goal or goals. Vision statements can be made for the entire company, for a department, and for individuals. They are usually expressed in "we will" (or "I will") language. For example, a company's vision statement might be any (or all) of the following:

- *We will* be a $100-million company by the year 2000

- *We will* have a broad base of customers with no single customer exceeding 3 percent of our annual revenue.

- *We will* service every zip code in the United States within the next five years,

- *We will* open ten new satellite offices within the next three years.

The vision statement of a division or department might be:

- *We will* have less than 5 percent quality defect rejection by 18 months from now.

- *We will* have a totally computerized inventory system within the next year.

And for an individual:

· *I will* be the number one salesperson (gross sales) within two years.

· *I will* be promoted to a senior management position within three years of starting to work for this company.

Notice, in each case, that the vision statement is a projection into the future. This expression of *where* a company, division, department, or individual wants to go is the distinguishing mark of a vision statement.

Mission Statements

A mission statement is a statement of *how* the vision will be achieved. It is a set of objectives to be accomplished in order to achieve the long-term goal(s). Functionally, the objectives serve as short-term goals. So a mission statement generally answers the questions. "How are we going to get there?" and "What has to be done to accomplish our vision?" Mission statements are typically stated in "by" language. For example: As a *company* we will attain our vision statement of being a $100-million company by the year 2000:

· *by* having the highest-quality products on the market.

· *by* having a better-trained sales force than all of the competition.

· *by* maintaining price advantage.

· *by* extending markets geographically into two new locations per year.

As a department, we will attain our vision of having less than 5 percent quality defect rejection within 18 months:

· *by* closely monitoring purchases and assuring quality control of purchased components.

· *by* rewarding workers for a combination of high quality and high production rather than high production alone.

As an individual, I will accomplish my vision statement of being promoted to a senior management position within three years:

· *by* ensuring that all reports are filled out on time.

· *by* presenting at least one new idea to management every month.

These are only a few examples of the kinds of issues to be addressed in order to put together an effective mission statement. The point here is that a mission statement defines *how* you are going to make your vision statement happen; it lists the steps you will take to bring your vision to reality.

Values Statements

Values statements exist on quite a different plane from vision and mission statements. A values statement expresses the *standards of behavior* to be followed by the people within a company as they work to bring their vision and mission statements to fruition. Vision and mission statements deal with *things to do;* values statements deal with *ways to do* those things.

By comparison. suppose you had a "to do" list. Let this be the equivalent of your mission statement. Now you ask yourself, "In what way will I do the things on the list?" For example, will you do them as fast as you can, as slowly as possible, or at a pace that feels comfortable to you? Will you do them carefully or recklessly? Will you strive for perfection on each of the tasks, or will you want only to complete them, regardless of quality? These are questions of value. Values statements answer the question, "What are the *rules for our behavior* as we proceed?"

Values Statements in the Workplace

Let's look at this in a business context. In dealing with customers, is our behavior going to be relaxed or formal, light or serious, friendly or aloof? Are we going to work so intensely toward our goals that we ask our employees to work forty-five hour weeks until our goals are achieved? Or will there be periods of play time and relaxation built in to renew our people along the way? Are we going to listen closely to what our customers tell us they need and respond accordingly, or are we going to project what we think the customer will need and gamble on our predictions?

As before, this is only. small sampling of the sorts of questions that must be addressed in putting together a values statement. The point here is that values statements deal with the question *"What is important to us in terms of our standard at behavior—our rules of conduct?"* as we move toward achieving the goals in our vision and mission statements.

Values Statements and Corporate Culture

Corporate culture, you will recall from Chapter 7, is: *The spoken and unspoken rules in an organization that set the standards for how things are to be done; the company ethos; the characteristics and distinguishing ways of thinking, feeling, and behaving in any given occupational group; the pervasive attitudes, values, beliefs, and actions of the people within a company.*

Values statements, as just discussed, are: *The standards of behavior in a company; the ways to do things in the workplace; the rules for conduct.*

It should now be clear that "corporate culture" and "values statements" are closely related concepts. The culture of a company is defined far more by its values statements than by its vision and mission statements. Corporate culture is the sum total of the values of a company.

Why Is This Distinction So Important?

Many companies are well-practiced at putting together vision statements and mission statements. Usually under the guidance of a trained consultant, and often at considerable expense, companies spend endless exhausting hours putting these statements together to guide them forward.

The mistake that many companies make is to assume that their culture is determined by their vision or mission statements. This is simply not the case.

Again, vision statements tell where a company is going. Mission statements—how you are going to get there—flow logically from the vision statement. Values statements, on the other hand, define the standards of behavior for getting to where you are going. They do not flow logically from either the vision or the mission statement. They are independent of the others. Values statements express an altogether different dimension of the corporate experience. They are codes of conduct to be superimposed over both vision and mission. In other words, values statements alone establish your culture.

We've said before that to rid your company of excuses, you must develop an excuse-free culture. We've also said that the way to do this is to manage excuses. What couldn't have been said with any degree of clarity until now is that *the only way to manage excuses effectively is to* **commit** *yourself to the values statement:* **This company will have an excuse-free culture.**

Why This Must Be Done Now

One of the big problems in corporate America today is that the rate of change in the business environment is much greater than it has ever been. And this rate of change is going to increase geometrically as technological development continues to accelerate and information becomes more and more readily available. The result is that too often vision and mission statements have little meaning in today's marketplace because of the tremendously fast changing conditions. By the time some vision and mission statements are put together. The business has so radically changed that the statements are no longer completely valid—if they are still valid at all.

This is not to say that vision and mission statements are no longer important. On the contrary, they remain a necessity. But they are not *as* important in today's business climate as a well-defined values statement.

For Instance

A company can have perfect vision and mission statements and yet fail miserably if the values statement creates a culture that cannot respond to fast-changing market conditions. Conversely, a company that may not have the perfect vision and mission statements but which has a solid values statement (and therefore a good culture of people) can succeed because of its responsiveness, proactivity, creativity, optimism, acceptance of responsibility, and so on.

Example #1

Let's suppose Company A has the following vision statement: We will have the most technologically superior products in the marketplace in five years. Its mission statement reads. We will accomplish this by introducing one new product every 12 months. Even though these statements may be otherwise realistic, the vision could crash if there is no values statement that guarantees a proactive mindset of the people in research and development. How can they ever become technologically superior as stated in the vision statement if their way of being—their standard of behavior—is *reactive*? By definition, reactive people are always at least one step behind whoever is in the lead. And, no doubt, they will have plenty of excuses for not being the most technologically superior, because where there is reactive thinking, there will be excuses. Always.

If excuses are not managed in an organization through a clear values statement that demands excuse-free behavior from its people, the culture will automatically default to the excuse-making syndrome. This will be true regardless of the clarity of the vision statement, and regardless of the specificity of the mission statement.

Example #2

Here is Company B with a vision statement of having customers in every zip code in the country by the year 2000. Its mission statement is to hire enough salespeople to accomplish that market coverage. But if in their rapid growth they hire salespeople who tend to externalize their failures ("It's someone else's fault") rather than internalize them ("It's my responsibility"), it is unlikely that the vision statement will ever be achieved.

This is because there is not a strong values statement that insists on internalization rather than externalization from its employees. The culture will be excuse-infested because the proper values statement is not in place that will drive excuses out of the culture. If and when the going gets tough, the people on the sales force will therefore likely be projecting blame and shirking responsibility rather than doing whatever is necessary to get the desired results. Externalization and excuses are kissing cousins. Externalization can only thrive in an excuse laden culture. And where there are excuses, there won't be results.

Conversely

Company C has a vision also: to be number one in the marketplace with their product line within the next four years. Their mission statement: to accomplish this by doing whatever it takes to achieve their vision. (This mission statement, by the way, would fail nearly every consultant's test—it's not specific, not measurable, and so on.)

Yet if company C's values statement is that it will have an excuse-free culture, then it will only hire people to he leaders who meet the criteria of leadership (according to the clear understanding of leadership as spelled out in Chapter 8). This means that the company will end up with a team of people who want the organization to be number one. Even though they may not have any idea at that point how they're going to make their vision a reality, the point is that the values of their people will be so strong—so excuse-free—that they will indeed become number one, whatever it takes to get there.

The strength of the core values of a company is closely tied to the strength of the leaders of that company. It is excuse-free leadership that allows this approach to work. However, excuse-free leadership is not something that just happens by itself. **It is something that must be aggressively pursued; and this aggressive pursuit flows directly out of the values statement of the company.**

The Point, Once Again

As we said, you should not conclude that vision and mission statements are useless. However, as you look to what the future of your company should be, it is important that you focus not only on products and services but also on developing and maintaining the proper culture.

The only culture that can respond to—and win in the marketplace is the culture that is proactive, creative, optimistic, responsible, accountable, stretching, trusting, helpful, focused, risk-taking, blame-accepting, internalizing, and so on. **This is the excuse-free culture that grows out of your commitment to an excuse-free values statement.**

This is the culture required to surge ahead of others and become the leader in the daily race of the marketplace. This is how to become number one again.

What to Do Next

At this point, you do not have to appoint special committees who will wrestle for months with the questions "How do we want our people to behave, and what do we want our values statement to be?" *Step one is simply a matter of committing yourself to adopting the values statement:* **This company will become excuse-free.** This is far more important than the development of your products and your services, your visions and your missions.

If you do this, your people will develop your business for you. By getting rid of excuses, you will foster all the positives that are the derivatives in an excuse-free envi-

143

ronment. And those positives will give you a corporate team that is strong enough to take your company to any height that you would like it to go, even to being (and remaining) number one.

Your Involvement Is Crucial

An excuse-free culture can only be achieved when those at the top express their commitment by (1) making the decision to proceed, and (2) actively involving themselves in the process. When this is not done, others in the organization will perceive the non-involvement of top management as a statement that achieving an excuse-free culture is unimportant (since actions speak louder than words). Also, any reason given for the non-involvement will be taken as an excuse in itself, whether or not it really is an excuse.

Either way, when it comes to eliminating excuses from the workplace, it will do little good to tell others to do something that you are not willing to be involved in yourself. *Real* commitment, remember, involves the willingness to change, the willingness to risk, the willingness to invest time, and the illingness to invest money. The third of these—the willingness to invest time—does not just mean the time of others. It means your time as well.

When it comes to ridding your company of excuses, direct and active involvement by the decision-maker(s) is mandatory. Right from the start it gives an important message to your people that you are serious in your commitment to bring your values statement to reality, and to have your company become excuse-free.

In Review

- **An excuse-free culture represents an ideal. The secret is not to become totally excuse-free as much as it is to *continuously strive for that ideal*. The closer a company comes to becoming excuse-free, the further it will move ahead of the pack,** outdistancing by far those who do little or nothing to manage excuses in their company.

· In order to accomplish *real* change, a company must be *ready* to change, must *want* to change, and must be *committed* to change.

· Being committed to anything means being willing to change, risk, invest time, and invest money.

· Establishing vision statements, mission statements, and values statements must be part of the planning process for all companies. Of the three, a company's values statement, far more than the other two, defines that company's culture.

· To win in today's economy, you must be committed to making your values statement the guiding light for action in your company, even more so than your vision and mission statements.

· Specifically, the values statement that you must commit yourself to is to become excuse-free.

· If you do this, you will automatically foster a corporate culture that attracts, develops, and keeps the people necessary to help your business grow. It will consist of a group of people who: insist on being in touch with the needs of the customer; are able to adjust quickly to a fast-changing business climate; are optimistic, proactive, courageous, risk-taking, and so on; and settle for nothing less than becoming number one again.

Notes and Quotes

Whoever wants to be a judge of human nature should study people's excuses.

Hebbel

CHAPTER 13

The Diagnostic Step: Are We Infected?

Once there is commitment at the top to develop an excuse-free culture, the next step is to determine to what degree your company is infected.

Before You Begin Your Diagnosis

We have made a point of saying that the culture of every corporation is unique to that company, just as personalities are unique to individuals. It is probably fair to say that no two companies have identical cultures.

But the question of how the culture – the collective values—of your company is unique from others is not the real issue here. The diagnostic question you need to focus on is: *To what degree is my unique culture infected with the excuse-making virus?* That is, to what extent are excuses and excuse-fostering behaviors manifesting themselves within my company?

This Is Really a Three-Part Question

Your company is made up of three distinct components: the organizational structure, the processes, and the people. The **organizational** component of a corporation is literally the way the company is organized. It is the organizational flow chart. It is the determination of what the various divisions and departments of the company are, and who reports to whom. The **processes** are the various systems used by the company to accomplish necessary tasks. For example, planning is accomplished through the planning process, employee evaluation through the evaluation process, and so on. The **people**, of course, are individuals who fill the positions within the company.

So the question "Are excuses manifesting themselves in my company?" is really three questions:

1. **"Does the organizational structure of my company create conditions under which people are allowed, encouraged, or 'forced' to make excuses?"**

2. **"Do any of the processes used in my company breed excuse-making behaviors?"**

3. **"After the organization and processes are fixed, are any of the people who work here still excuse-makers, *especially* those in leadership positions?"**

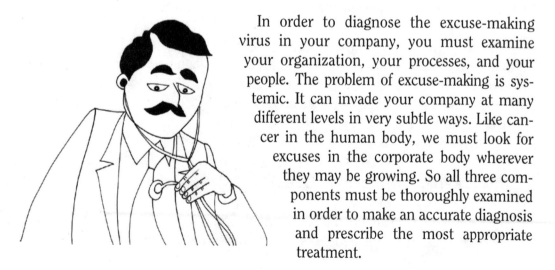

In order to diagnose the excuse-making virus in your company, you must examine your organization, your processes, and your people. The problem of excuse-making is systemic. It can invade your company at many different levels in very subtle ways. Like cancer in the human body, we must look for excuses in the corporate body wherever they may be growing. So all three components must be thoroughly examined in order to make an accurate diagnosis and prescribe the most appropriate treatment.

Technically speaking, the organizational and process components of your company cannot *make* excuses; only people can do that. But the organization and the processes can have built-in weaknesses that encourage excuse-making, just as a weakened immune system allows viruses to spread through the body. So when we talk about examining your organizational structure and your processes, we aren't really looking for excuses, but rather for the weakened condition—the context—in which excuses happen.

The Rule

In order to get rid of excuses, you must first get rid of the reasons why people make them. You must implement a systematic approach to change your company into an *extraordinary* organization with *extraordinary* processes in order to get *extraordinary* performance out of or dinary people.

So the rule is: ***Never start your diagnosis at the "people" level.*** *You can't know which excuses are related to individuals until you know which ones result from the organization and the processes.*

Approach the Diagnostic Process with an Open Mind

We cannot emphasize enough how difficult it can be to recognize the problematic nature of excuses as such. Seeing what's really there is one of the toughest jobs you'll have to do. *This is not because excuse-making is inherently difficult to see.* In fact, once you know how to spot it, it is quite easy to identify.

The problem is that we tend to be blind to excuses because of our perspective. When we're inside a paradigm, it's almost impossible to see outside of it—that is, to look at it objectively. This relates to our discussion in Chapter 6 about beliefs. For example, if we believe that everything that can be invented has been, we'll be ready to close the patent office. The point is that we tend to see only those things that fit inside the parameters of our paradigm.

149

A Common Example

Ron, the northwestern regional sales manager for a large retail fitness equipment company, asked Pete, one of his 16 salespeople, to prepare a proposal for a sizeable commercial job. The prospective customer was eager to get the job installed for their grand opening. The day before the proposal was due for Ron's approval, Pete asked for another two weeks because he had "simply been too busy to get to the proposal."

The "I'm too busy" excuse is one that is used commonly in the workplace. One of the reasons it is so often used—and generally so quickly accepted by others—is that it is seen from inside a specific paradigm that *busyness is a positive thing*. Think about when you ask someone, "How are you?" Often the response is "Busy." This is a respectable answer. Perhaps it's a carry over from the Protestant work ethic: that hard work is good, and if you're busy, you must be working hard. Whatever the reason, the commonly accepted paradigm in our society, and therefore in our companies, is that busyness is a virtue. Besides, it is easy enough to identify with the person who says, "I'm too busy," because we're all so busy most of the time ourselves.

But this is exactly the point. When we are inside of the "busyness is a virtue" paradigm, it is very difficult to have another perspective. Yet outside of that paradigm is another reality, the proposal is not completed on time, the competition may have just gained a huge competitive edge, and the deal may be lost. Worse than that, the prospective customer's trust may have eroded because what was said would be done in a certain time frame wasn't *in fact* done. This may negatively impact any attempt to get future business with the firm—and perhaps even with others if the word gets out that this fitness equipment company doesn't make good on its promises.

A Reminder

Remember what we said in the Preface about how little material we were able to find on the subject of excuses. Information about excuses is conspicuously missing from the literature. This could only happen in the context—the paradigm—that excuses are *not* all that important and certainly *not* all that destructive.

But outside of that paradigm is another possibility. That possibility is exactly the new management theory we are advancing in this book: *Excuses are extremely important; they wreak havoc in our corporations when it comes to getting results; and they stand in the way of recapturing our number-one position in the marketplace.*

Switching Paradigms

We are asking you to step from one paradigm, where excuses and their relatives are mostly ignored, into another paradigm—the opposite one, really—where you realize that excuse-making causes problems almost every where you look. Making this shift isn't easy to do. It takes a little time, a little patience, and a lot of open-mindedness.

And yet, the elimination of excuses from the workplace is not all that difficult once you recognize (i.e., diagnose) the real problem. *It is in the recognition of the size of the problem that your first major challenge lies.*

So look closely with open eyes and with an open mind as you proceed with your diagnosis, or you may miss what there is to see. Keep your eyes open to new possibilities, or you may inadvertently slip back into the old paradigm where the chances of distorting the accuracy of your diagnosis are high.

The Audit as a Diagnostic Tool

Traditionally, problems in corporations have been identified by means of the audit. The purpose of the audit is to work through a checklist of questions to determine whether and where your company may need help. The most prevalent is the financial audit. Also high on the list is the audit where procedural efficiency is examined. There are other audits as well: security audits (which study the security of data in computer systems), billing-record audits, etc.

The Traditional Audit Won't Work to Diagnose Excuses

Audits are very useful tools for identifying certain kinds of problems. They look at hard data—data that are specific, objective, factual, measurable, and usually numerical, such as dollars in sales, days missed on the job, profit margins, material costs, and employee turnover.

The problem is that a company's culture, its collective value system, is *not* hard data. It is intangible and therefore more subjective than objective. It is the manifestation of human behavior within the corporation, and human behavior is "soft" data, not hard. This is why the traditional audit will not be effective for diagnosing the excuse-making virus in your company.

The 360-Degree Audit

The key to accurate diagnosis of anything that is intangible and subjective is to look at it from as many different angles as possible. This is why there are several members on a jury. The accuracy of the judgment for or against the defendant lies in the collective perception. It is the same reason that we have judges in such sporting events as boxing, diving, gymnastics, and horse shows. Usually the judges place themselves at different angles to the event. They need to see it from as many perspectives as possible to insure accuracy.

So it is with the 360-degree audit. It is a valuable tool because the accuracy of the score is based on the concept that the aggregate perception is the one closest to reality. Upper management, for example, will see something from one perspective, middle management from quite another, and line workers from still another.

Which brings to mind a fable by John Godfrey Saxe (Stevenson, 1953) to help make this point:

> · **It was six men of Indostan, to learning much inclined.**
> **Who went see the Elephant (though all of them were blind)**
> **That each by observation could satisfy his mind.**

- The first approached the Elephant, and happening to fall
  Against his broad and sturdy side, at once began to bawl:
  "God bless me! but the Elephant is very much like a wall!"

- The second, feeling of the tusk, cried "Ho! what have we here
  So very round and smooth and sharp? To me 'tis mighty clear
  This wonder of an Elephant is very like a spear!"

- The third approached the animal, and happening to take
  The squirming trunk within his hands, thus boldly up and spake:
  "I see," quoth he, "the Elephant is very like a snake!"

- The fourth reached out on eager hand, and felt about the knee.
  "What most this wondrous beast is like is mighty plain," quoth he:
  "Tis clear enough the Elephant is very like a tree!"

- The fifth who chanced to touch the ear, said: "E'en the blindest man
  Can tell what this resemble most: deny the fact who can,
  This, marvel of on Elephant is very like a fan!"

- The sixth no sooner had began about the beast to grope,
  Than, seizing on the winging tail that fell within his scope,
  "I see," quoth he, "the Elephant is very like a rope!"

- And so these men of Indostan disputed loud and long,
  Each in his own opinion exceeding stiff and strong,
  Though each was partly in the right, and all were in the wrong!

The Point

Two important things are accomplished by the 360 degree audit. First, it prevents the "wrong"—or more precisely, the *narrowness*—that can result from any single perspective in the corporate environment. Second, it takes all the "partly rights" and, by putting them all together, it collectively builds the most accurate picture. That is

153

why the 360° is such a necessary and valuable diagnostic tool.

Whereas the 360 degree can be used in many different ways to measure corporate behaviors, it is crucial that you use it to diagnose the excuse-making syndrome in your organization. Remember, excuses and their partners are next to impossible to identify in ourselves. They are designed to protect, and are therefore invisible to those being protected. You must rely on the collective perception to spot both excuses and the weaknesses in the system which allow them to grow.

In figure 10 (p. 166) we will introduce you to a sample 360 audit that you can use to diagnose excuse-making in your company. There are some other things, however, that need to be discussed first.

The 360° Audit Isn't New, but When, Where, and How to Use It, Is

Three-sixty surveys are becoming common practice in companies. Almost all of the 360's currently in use survey specific individuals. That's fine. *But in order to get rid of excuses you must survey your organization and your processes first.* Again, with regard to eliminating excuses from the workplace, **never start your diagnosis at the "people" level.** *You can't know which excuses are related to individuals until you know which ones result from the organization and the processes.*

The Importance of Anonymity

For the 360 audit to work effectively as a diagnostic tool, those who participate in it must be guaranteed anonymity if they desire it. Otherwise people will be frightened of the process and will not furnish accurate information. Since in the first stage you are looking for information about your organization and your processes rather than your people, knowing specific names isn't necessary. So don't require them.

In some companies, people will insist that they want names on all 360's. When this happens, it can force a lot of introspection, progressive thinking, and benefits.

But only if that is what *everyone* wants. Putting names on the surveys can be a choice, but in the first stage it is clearly not necessary.

The Clear Understanding of Purpose

Everyone must be given a clear understanding of the purpose of the survey. There can be no mystery about it, or people will feel uneasy.

The purpose of the 360° diagnosis in the beginning stage is to assess accurately to what degree your organization and your processes allow the excuse-making virus to live and spread in your company. It is *not* to identify certain individuals as being excuse-makers.

You want your people to feel safe so they will be totally objective and give you accurate information about your organization and your processes. To accomplish this, make sure that (a) no one is required to put his or her name on the 360° diagnostic sheets; (b) people are reassured that the purpose is not to hurt anyone, but to eliminate excuses from the workplace so that the company will be as healthy as possible; and (c) the information is processed by an outside, objective firm.

Whom To Include in the 360

Again, the purpose of the diagnostic step is to determine at what levels and to what degree your organization and your processes are infected with excuses. To insure an accurate diagnosis, it is important to seek a summary of observations from several levels both inside and outside of your company. You need to include at least these four levels in your 360 diagnosis:

- **Oneself**
- **Leadership/Management Team**
- **Employees**
- **Outside Sources**

Each of these layers is distinct and provides a valuable perspective. Let's look at each category.

Oneself

We mean a diagnosis, not _on_ oneself, but rather _by_ the "top dog" in any given unit. His 360° survey will be _on_ the organization and the processes within that unit. If the unit being diagnosed is the entire company, this would be by the owner, president, or CEO. If the unit being diagnosed is the division of a company, it would be by whoever is in charge of that division, such as the division manager. If the unit under observation is a satellite office, it would be by whoever directs that office, such as the branch manager.

Leadership/Management Team

Here, again, we mean _by_, not _on_, everyone who is in a leadership or management position. What your leaders and managers will be surveying is the organization and the processes in the unit being diagnosed. Depending on the number of people involved, it may be helpful to divide this group into various levels of management, such as upper and middle management, department heads, line supervisors, and so on, to get the unique perspective of each level.

Employees

This would include anyone who is not in a position of management or supervision. If the company is small enough and if the numbers are manageable, it would be best to have every employee do a 360 evaluation on the organization and the processes. The larger the company, the more important it will be to randomly sample the various populations of workers. Of course, the larger the number of employees surveyed, the more accurate the collective perception.

Outside Sources

To elicit the most accurate response from outside sources about your organization and your processes, they must be clearly informed as to what you are trying to accomplish. This takes courage on your part. Many companies have struggled with this because they hate admitting their weaknesses, especially to their customers. The irony is, your customers are probably more aware of your weaknesses than you *or* your company are. It's just that, in the end, customers have a peculiar way of telling you: They just quit calling.

Which Outside Sources to Select

There are any number of external sources you might go to for help on the 360. In some ways, these outside agents can furnish the most valuable information of all. How those outside your company view your organization and your processes may speak the loudest as to the presence or absence of excuses in your company.

Possible sources include: suppliers, customers, banks or other financial institutions with which you do business, prospective employees, former employees, competitors, other business leaders, community leaders, and community members. Which of these to invite into the project will depend on the size and location of your company, availability of outside agents, and the appropriateness of each to your particular situation. Obviously, it would be impractical—and unnecessary for a company of any size to approach all such sources. The rule again is this: Within reason, *the broader the base of perception, the more accurate the diagnosis*. Also, the larger the company, the more likely it is that a random sampling will suffice.

As before, those outsiders who agree to help furnish the information must be totally protected by making their 360's anonymous and confidential.

A Useful Rating Form for the 360

Figure 10 (p. 166) is a rating form you can use to get the initial raw data you will need to make an accurate diagnosis. The list is a small representation. There will be many items that you need to add or delete, depending on your circumstances. You will notice that the items listed are excuse-related behaviors (for example, projection of blame, procrastination, and so on) rather than excuses themselves. The reason, remember, is that excuses can disguise themselves in many different ways, so we need to look for as many of those disguises as possible.

You will also notice that the items are the same ingredients that were listed in the body of the iceberg beneath the surface of the water in Chapter 5. These are the problems that tend to hang around each other in companies. They are "birds of a feather that flock together." They all "go with" each other. Where you find one, you will almost always find the others. They are like metastasized cells of the same colony of cancer. Just as cancer cells live at the expense of everything else around them, so excuses and their relatives live at the expense of other life-giving qualities in an organization. *Your diagnosis must attempt to isolate **every** cell, or recurrence of the problem is inevitable.*

Application of the 360 Survey

This particular audit has a broad application. It can be used to survey any part of the organization, from its entirety down to any division, satellite, branch, or department. It can also be used to audit any process within the company, the planning process, the hiring process, the evaluation and promotion process, the sales and marketing process, the process of setting individual goals, and so on.

To repeat: It can also be used to survey individuals if and when the time is right to do that. It is never the right time to survey individuals in the early stages of the diagnostic process. It is far more important to diagnose the organizational structure and the processes first so as to eliminate the reasons that people make excuses. Many excuses will begin to go away when the reasons that people make excuses are eliminated.

360 Organizational and Process Survey

Organization or Process under Audit:

Directions

Circle one number for each category that most applies to the organization or process being surveyed (Read each item as if it were preceded by whichever of the following words is most appropriate: **"encourages" "allows," or "forces.")**:

Acceptance of blame	4	3	2	1	Projection of blame
Non-entitlement attitudes	4	3	2	1	Entitlement attitudes
Proactive thinking	4	3	2	1	Reactive thinking
Can-do attitudes	4	3	2	1	Can't-do attitudes
Effective teamwork	4	3	2	1	Ineffective teamwork
Optimism	4	3	2	1	Pessimism
Taking risks	4	3	2	1	Not taking risks
Competence	4	3	2	1	Incompetence
Respectfulness	4	3	2	1	Disrespectfulness
Confronting of issues	4	3	2	1	Avoidance of issues
Being focused	4	3	2	1	Being unfocused
Empowerment	4	3	2	I	Helplessness
Being realistic with self	4	3	2	1	Being self-deceitful
Do-it-now attitudes	4	3	2	1	Procrastination
Results orientation	4	3	2	1	Excuse orientation
Creativeness	4	3	2	1	Non-creativeness
Stretching (to meet commitments)	4	3	2	I	Not stretching (to meet commitments)
Trust	4	3	2	1	Distrust
Harmonious relationships	4	3	2	1	Conflictual relationships
Courage to fail	4	3	2	1	Fear of failure
Accountability	4	3	2	1	Non-accountability
Leading	4	3	2	I	Following
Personal power to make Change happen	4	3	2	1	Victimization
Acceptance of responsibility	4	3	2	1	Denial or responsibility
Long-term focus	4	3	2	1	Short-term focus

Scoring the Surveys

There are 25 items on this representative list. A perfect score (which would indicate the most excuse-free environment) on each survey would be 100—4 points on each item times 25 items. The worst score possible (which would indicate the presence of the most number of excuses) would be 25—1 point on each item times 25 items.

Remember, however, that the final rating will be a composite score based on the averages of all people involved in the exercise *within a certain category or class of people* taking it (the classes being "oneself," "leadership management," "employees," and "outside sources"). Since each category of people participating in the survey has its own unique perspective of the problem, lumping all the scores from all the classes together could contaminate the accuracy of the diagnosis.

Interpreting the Data

There should be some cause for concern *any time* the score is less than perfect (that is, any average score of less than 100). This signals that there is the *perception* that excuses are at work somewhere in your organization or your processes, even if in a small way. *Every perception is a piece of the whole reality*. It is like the elephant fable. Any single perception of the elephant was not the "real" or "whole" elephant. But it was a *piece* of the real elephant, and, as such, it had definite merit.

The point is, where there is the *perception* that the excuse-making virus is at work in your organization or your processes, then *it is* at work to some degree. If it looks like a duck and quacks like a duck, it probably is a duck. It must therefore be given immediate attention. It would be the equivalent of diagnosing and treating cancer in its earliest stages. This will greatly reduce the chance that the disease of excuse-making will spread.

The Rule for Interpreting Your Surveys

The lower the score, the bigger the problem. Anything less than a perfect score indicates that the excuse-making virus is at work in your company. The lower the score, the more of a hold the virus has on your organization. The higher the score, the less of a hold it has.

The concept of "being number one again" means that companies must strive toward the goal of being 100 percent excuse-free. Remember the starting point of this book: *Where there are excuses, there will be less than the desired results. Conversely, where there are the desired results, there will not be excuses. It is a contradiction of terms to have any excuses operating in your corporation and still be functioning at 100 percent effectiveness. Whether it is people, teams, companies, or countries: those who are number one have no room and no time for excuses. They are totally invested in getting results.*

What Is an "Acceptable" Score?

What level of performance are you satisfied with? Are you content to lead a company that is below average, average, above average—or are you driven to become (and remain) number one? There is one thing you can count on: *Winners strive to become number one. A score of 100 **is** number one. And when you're number one, you can't help but win!*

The End Result of the Diagnosis

As a result of the 360 surveys, you have determined to what degree your organization or your processes are infected with excuse-making. Your next job is to intervene in such a way that you will reverse the tendency in your company to unknowingly encourage, tolerate, or in some cases, even "force" people to make excuses. Doing this will help tremendously to overcome the excuse-making syndrome in your company, and to put you well on the road to recovery.

CHAPTER **14**

The Intervention Step: Lead or Get Out of the Way

Once the diagnoses of your organization and your processes are completed, you will know whether intervention is needed and, if so, where. Intervention is needed wherever there is the perception that excuses exist. This is because, by intervening in the excuse-making process, you are at the same time intervening in the destructive work of the many relatives of excuses as well: reactive thinking, projection of blame, pessimism, can't-do-attitudes, denial of responsibility, and so on. And with the elimination of these negatives comes a happier, more efficient place to work; pride of achievement; cooperative relationships where everyone pulls their own weight; competitive products and services; and higher profits.

Intervention Begins with Leaders

You will recall from the chapter on leadership (Chapter 8) that *it is the responsibility of leaders to furnish the impetus necessary to establish and maintain an excuse-free culture.*

So any discussion about intervening to turn around the excuse-making process must start with an evaluation of your leaders. This is the essential difference between the diagnostic step and the intervention step: The focus now turns from organization and processes to people—specifically, to the leaders.

The question now becomes: Are the leaders of the unit in question capable of making the change of taking the people from excuse-making to excuse-free behavior? It is not to be automatically assumed that present leaders have the necessary qualities. They may or they may not.

Remember, it takes specific leadership qualities to lead others into excuse-free behavior. It cannot be taken for granted that the people who are now in positions of management are up to the task. Leadership and management are two different concepts. It is a huge mistake to equate them. Leadership *"leads change,"* and management *"manages policy,"* i.e., *the status quo*. Are the people in the targeted department—those who will be called on to make the changes – leaders, or are they managers only?

The Point

You are looking for highly specific leadership qualities that are necessary for the task of achieving an excuse-free culture. If the unit targeted for intervention is the entire company, the people at the top levels must be assessed to determine whether or not they have these qualities. If the unit in question is a department or a division of the company, then the people in charge must be evaluated.

The purpose is not to chastise individuals, nor to set them up for embarrassment. It is to identify where the shortcomings are in your leaders so the problems can be corrected. You will recall that two of the qualities you need in your leaders are to be mentally tough and emotionally stable. True leaders are strong enough to look at the truth about themselves. They welcome the feedback about any behavior that is excuse-related so they can eliminate it. As Harry Truman said, "If you can't stand the heat, get out of the kitchen." If your "leaders" can't deal with the results of being evaluated for excuse-making, maybe that's a big clue that they aren't the type of leader you need.

Again, **if you want an excuse-free culture, leadership is where it all begins.** This is the cornerstone of the entire excuse-free concept.

Getting Started

There are two central questions to ask in the intervention step:

· **Do the people in charge of the targeted unit have the qualities necessary to lead the unit into an excuse-free culture?**

· **If the answer is "no," what can be done to remedy the situation?**

Are your Leaders Qualified?

The first way to determine the qualifications of your leaders is through your own observation. You need to begin to look at your leaders in a new way, through the filter of the leadership qualities that are required to lead others into excuse-free behaviors. These qualities are listed for you in figure 11 (p. 177).

Observe the leaders of each unit that needs intervention (as determined in the diagnostic step). Start by observing them in meetings. Instead of leading the meeting yourself, just sit in on it. Don't say anything, but rather look, listen, and learn. Use figure 11 as a checklist of behaviors. Observe each of your executives, managers, supervisors, or whomever you expect to be in positions of leadership in that unit. See in what ways these individuals do, or do not, manifest the qualities necessary to lead excuse-free behaviors in others.

You should, of course, observe them in settings other than just meetings—in the hallways, in one-on-one and small—group discussions, over the telephone, and so on. But the meeting room is an excellent place to begin because it allows you the quiet opportunity to focus on your leaders in a new way. It will make you better able to spot certain qualities and behaviors outside the meeting room.

A Helpful Hint

One thing to keep in mind during your observations: If you want to know what the true leadership qualities of an individual are, don't just listen to what he says. Focus on what he does. For example, the person in question may *say* he has a guiding vision, but you want to know whether or not he really has one, and the way to find out is to look for evidence *in his behavior*. Does he make others aware of what his vision is? Does he maintain a steady course in the achievement of a vision? Is his behavior consistent with his vision? These are the types of questions you must ask yourself about his behavior.

If a picture is worth a thousand words, one's behavior is worth ten thousand words, or more.

166

Using the 360° Survey Again

The second way to get at the question "Do our leaders have the necessary qualities?" is through the use of the 360° survey. Many times in our consulting practices we have seen examples of individuals who thought they were doing well, while the people around them had a very different opinion. The 360° survey is an effective, non-threatening tool for discovering such differences, because the subject is observed from several points of view.

It is often true in the workplace that the perception of a person or situation is more important than the reality about that person or situation. For example, suppose the reality is that a person is not involved in excuse-making behavior. But the perception by others is that the person is indeed guilty of such behavior. Something is out of sync here. At the very least, there is a problem with the extent or style of communication. The point is, *while perception may not always accurately identify the nature of a problem, it always reflects the reality that **there is** a problem.*

Anonymously and confidentially, you will want to ask people at various levels about their perceptions of the leader or leaders in question. Remember that you want to multiply the angles of perception to insure greater accuracy of your results. The greater the number of perceptions, the closer you get to the reality of the qualities of your "leaders."

Again, perceptual differences are differences that need to be resolved. It doesn't matter who's right or who's wrong, but rather what the differences are in perception. In other words, if person A thinks he's a good leader, and person B disagrees, it doesn't matter if person A is right or if person B is right. It only matters that something be done to ensure that both, or neither, come to see person A as a good leader. *If there is a perceived problem, there is a problem. Positive results come from aligned perceptions. Otherwise, resistance to all attempts to move forward is inevitable.*

Who Should Be Given the 360°?

You need to involve four different groups of people in the 360° surveys:

- **The leaders in the unit or units where intervention is necessary**
- **All executives who rank above that level of leadership in the organization, if any**
- **Employees within the unit**
- **Other leaders within the company who rank laterally with the leaders in question**

True Leaders Get Rid of Excuses

Keep in mind here that your single focus is to evaluate leadership in terms of those characteristics that either *encourage and breed excuses* in the workplace or *discourage and eliminate excuses*. Nothing more. It's that simple. When excuses go, results happen. So you need to find out whether or not you have those players in leadership positions who can get rid of excuses.

The Leadership 360°

The leadership qualities listed in this survey are the exact ones that were spelled out in Chapter 8. Figure 11 is a rating form that you can use to determine whether or not an individual meets the requirements to lead his unit into excuse-free behavior.

360° Leadership Survey

Unit or person being surveyed:_____

Directions: Circle the most appropriate number for each category where 4 = outstanding, 3 = good, 2 = fair, 1 = poor

Has a guiding vision	4	3	2	1
Respects a higher authority	4	3	2	1
Is self-confident	4	3	2	1
Is enthusiastic	4	3	2	1
Has a high energy level	4	3	2	1
Focuses on the big picture	4	3	2	1
Is intuitive & makes decisions inductively	4	3	2	1
Expects success from self and others	4	3	2	1
Is self-disciplined	4	3	2	1
Is willing to take risks	4	3	2	1
Is mentally tough & emotionally stable	4	3	2	1
Submits to the need for additional knowledge	4	3	2	1
Is a good listener	4	3	2	1
Is "lucky"	4	3	2	1
Is introspective	4	3	2	1
Has personal integrity	4	3	2	1
Has control	4	3	2	1
Is decisive	4	3	2	1
Is a good communicator	4	3	2	1
Is sensitive to others' feelings and sense of dignity	4	3	2	1

Figure 9

The score on each survey is calculated by adding the circled numbers. There are 20 items with a possible score of 4 on each item. The highest score possible, therefore, would be 80, and the lowest would be 20.

Interpreting the Data

The goal is to bring all of your leaders to 100 percent leadership capabilities (that is, a score of 80 on the 360° survey). Our experience is that some people are more demanding than others, and some are more lenient, in the way they assess their leaders. So it is difficult to say exactly what score separates leaders from non-leaders.

A useful way to handle this difficulty is to start with the individuals who have the lowest scores, regardless of what those scores happen to be. Clearly, these people represent your biggest challenge in terms of developing an excuse-free culture. Your job is to make an important decision about each of them. Do you:

· **develop the necessary leadership qualities in these individuals through specific training programs?**

· **reposition people within your company to ensure that you have individuals with higher scores in the leadership positions in that unit?**

· **let individuals with the lowest scores go and hire new people who have the necessary qualities?**

Developing the Necessary Qualities

You may have noticed that some of the leadership qualities lend themselves to development more than others.

For example, it is probably easier for a person to improve his communication skills than to enhance his personal integrity. This is not to say that one's integrity can't be developed, but rather that the task may be more difficult. It depends partly on the person in question.

The point is, to help you decide whether or not to begin developing the necessary leadership qualities in a particular person, you will need to look at *which* qualities need improving, and contrast this against the personality of the individual. There are many variables involved, so it is difficult to furnish a handy checklist to accomplish this. In the end, whether or not to work with your people to help them develop leadership qualities is a judgment call. One way you can come up with a clearer answer is to go ahead with training and then determine which individuals have improved and to what degree.

The Importance of Measuring The Results of Training Your Leaders

If you decide to proceed with training, *you must make sure that you measure the results of the training* to see whether you are, in fact, developing the necessary characteristics required of your leaders. If they make progress as a result of the training, then you know that you made the right decision to keep them. If not, then you may need to reconsider.

One of the failings of training programs in general is the absence of effective methods to measure the results. It's like training a distance runner without ever having access to a stopwatch. How would you know if the athlete is improving his performance? Likewise, how would you know whether or not the training programs you are using are bringing you the desired results?

Typically what happens with training and development is that somebody first recognizes there is a problem. Then they bring in a specialist to work on that problem, with no predetermined measurement at the beginning and no measurement at the conclusion. Often the training, and the results of the training, are disappointing.

This frustration and waste of resources (or perceived waste of resources) can be greatly mitigated by doing pre and post-measurements. *No training program is worthwhile unless the results can be measured against some standard of success.*

This is why the 360° is such a tremendous tool. Its periodic use helps to determine whether or not progress has been made against predetermined weaknesses. This is how you can know in the long run whether to keep someone in a position of leadership, reposition him, or let him go. Your decision in the beginning doesn't have to be the perfect decision; it only has to be the right decision in the end.

Repositioning Your Leaders

It is quite possible that you have certain leaders in your company who do an outstanding job of demanding no-option, excuse-free behavior. They may just not be used to calling it that. In some cases, it may make sense to move one or more such individuals to the key leadership positions where help is needed. Remember from the last chapter that the purpose of the diagnostic step is to identify where and to what degree your organization or your processes are infected. The results of your diagnosis would indicate where you might want to move some of your stronger leaders.

For the persons being replaced, you will need to determine if they can be moved to other positions. Remember, **a person can be a very effective manager without necessarily being an effective leader.** To transplant someone from one position to another so that a stronger leader can take his place is not to say that he isn't a strong manager. This should have no more stigma than moving a tight end to tackle to make sure you have the right people in the right positions on your team. Tackles and tight ends are both valuable and indispensible, but the skills required of the players at each position vary considerably.

Hiring New Leaders

Letting people go and hiring others to replace them is one of the more unpleasant tasks of corporate life. Still, it is sometimes necessary. To *get results, not excuses,* you cannot compromise ensuring that you have the right people in leadership positions.

When you find it necessary to get rid of someone in a leadership position because of his inability or unwillingness to practice excuse-free behavior and demand it of others, you yourself are being a leader. You are a prime example of practicing what you preach: Your **guiding vision** (to rid your company of excuse-making) is an act of **respecting a higher authority** (the authority of your values statement). It is part of **staying focused on the big picture** and not letting obstacles (i.e. the wrong person in a position of leadership) get in the way. It is an expression **of expecting success from self and others** in that success is defined as becoming excuse-free. It is an act of **mental toughness and emotional stability** to let someone go who is not suited for the assignment. It also means that you are **in control** and **decisive.** *The leadership qualities that you model when you let a person go and hire another to replace him are the very leadership qualities you expect from others.*

As for actually hiring new people into leadership positions, it will of course be absolutely necessary to hire individuals who have the characteristics of leadership as listed in figure 11 and as discussed in Chapter 8. It will do little good to fire certain individuals, only to replace them with people who are no more capable of leading than those whom you let go. The specific skills and tools required to hire leaders who can lead others into excuse-free behavior is a topic too large to cover at this time. It will, however, be explored in detail in a future work.

In Conclusion

Ridding your company (or department or unit) of excuses is your primary task. That process begins and ends in leadership. It cannot be accomplished without the right players. Your leaders must be individuals who can lead in the direction of an excuse-free culture. If that means intervention is necessary to train, reposition, or replace certain persons, then that's what must be done. You are not looking to run a popularity contest, or to be seen by everyone as Mr. Nice Guy. Your job is to *get results, not excuses* in order to become number one again. Nothing short of that should matter.

If you want to get results, not excuses, you must find the right people for the leadership positions in your company. This is your number-one priority in the intervention step.

CHAPTER 15

The Integration Step: Developing a Unified System

One of Total Quality Management's most fundamental principles is the importance of integrating the vision and mission statements with the personal goals of everyone in the company. Few would argue that the TQM approach is valid. Those companies that have applied it have realized that a high level of commitment is necessary to reap its benefits.

The TQM approach is not far removed from what we mean by the concept of integration. The difference is that TQM integrates the *vision* and *mission* statements into everyone's personal goals with the single focus being *quality*. Our system of management integrates the values statement into everyone's personal goals with the single focus being *excuse-free behavior*. These two approaches—or for that matter, ours and any other management approach—are not to be seen in contest with each other. TQM, as with other management theories, emphasizes tasks—*things to do*; our system emphasizes behaviors—*ways to do those things*.

In this sense, we look at our management system as "beyond" TQM. We don't mean by this "better than", but rather, that excuse-free behavior *enhances* the quest for quality. *When you have the proper behavior, everything else you're striving to accomplish improves*, including quality.

How Does a Company "Integrate" an Excuse-Free Culture?

Your values statement *is* your desired culture. It must become part of everything you do. Your primary values statement, remember, is *to become excuse-free*. So the question that must be asked of all behavior in your company is, "Is this consistent with our goal to eliminate excuses from the workplace?"

The point is that virtually everything you do must be filtered through the asking —and the answering—of this question. In other words, when we set up our organizational structure, when we develop our processes, when we deal with our people—are we doing this in a way that supports excuse-free behavior?

Let's look at a few examples of what it means to integrate each of these elements—organization, processes, and people.

Integration of Your Organization

One company we worked with was a two-part company: a multi-location retail operation and a single-location wholesale operation. The company made an attempt at vertical integration by having the wholesale part of their company be the sole supplier for their retail operations. What happened is that the retailers began to complain that they couldn't make any money because wholesale was charging them too much. Wholesale claimed that they were charging that much because retail wouldn't let them sell outside of their organization. This was artificially keeping their sales level low, so they had to charge more. Naturally, this projection of blame onto each other led to a good deal of infighting because—structurally speaking—this represented a major organizational problem. Since the rewards of both parts of the company were based on sales, the company was set up organizationally to cause dissention, projection of blame, denial of responsibility, externalization, and therefore necessarily, excuses. This is a fairly common example of how the structure of the organization is not integrated with a values statement to have an excuse-free culture. Any time this is the case, one of two things is true: either there is no values statement to become excuse-free; or the values statement to become excuse-free is in place, but the organization won't allow for that value to be integrated.

In this particular case, the second was true, That is, the company had a values statement in place to become excuse-free, and they believed in it, But the company was blocked in its effort to achieve its goal until the structure of their organization was repaired. They needed to decide what business they were in, wholesale or retail. And when they did, excuse-making went away and the desired results began to happen.

The thrust of the integration step is:
(1) to adopt the values statement to become excuse-free
(2) to make certain that it can be applied; and that no blocks exist or are allowed in the effort to implement it.

Integration at Your Processes

There are many examples that could be used here because companies typically have multiple processes. Some examples include:

- **the human resource process**

- **the process of developing individual goals**

- **the sales process**

- **the marketing process**

- **the invoicing process**

- **the financial statement process**

- **the product development process**

- **the purchasing process**

- **the customer service process**

- **the problem-solving process**

We will use only the first example—the human resource process—to look at integration. Specifically, let's look at the hiring, training, evaluation, and promotion portions of the human resource process.

1. **When hiring:** Are people screened against the backdrop of excuse-making? Are they asked questions that relate to their own personal values to see if they are consistent or inconsistent with being excuse-free? Do you know what questions to ask to find out if their personal values are excuse-free? Is there a company policy about expectations of results-oriented rather than excuse-oriented behavior? Is this communicated clearly to them? Are there clear penalties for excuse-making in your company, and are the interviewees told what those penalties are?

2. **Concerning training:** Are your training programs geared toward the elimination of excuses? Are periodic measurements and accountabilities built into the training process? Are those people who are discovered through employee evaluations to be making excuses specifically taught how to reverse their behavior? Are training programs in place that explain why people make excuses? Are there programs to help people deal more effectively with those who make excuses? Are training programs that contradict the excuse-free effort eliminated or modified? Are leaders taught how to lead others into excuse-free behavior?

3. **Regarding evaluations and incentives:** Are employee evaluations tailored to assess one's performance based on excuse-free standards? Are employees' incentives—whether recognition, pay raise, or promotion—based on their excuse-free behavior? Are promotions given on the basis of survival and seniority, or are they the consequence of clear and accurate measurement of results due to the absence of excuses in one's work-related behavior? Remember, where there are no excuses, there will be results.

Integration of Your People

This relates directly to the leadership issue. We've talked about how instrumental your leaders are to the development of an excuse-free culture. They alone furnish the impetus to turn around the behaviors in an excuse-infected company.

So the question needs to be asked. "Do the people you have in leadership positions have the qualities necessary to lead your company into excuse-free behavior?" This, you will recall, was the primary focus of the intervention step. If your "leaders" are excuse-makers themselves or are not focused on leading others into an excuse-free environment, then you have not yet properly integrated your people.

In addition, _everyone_ must have some of the same qualities that your leaders have, even if they are not in direct leadership positions. For example, all employees must respect a higher authority, be self-disciplined, be good listeners, and have personal integrity, your values statement to become excuse-free can't be fully integrated into your people until all your employees have developed the leadership skills that apply individually to themselves.

The Company That Pulls Together Wins Together

Every company, large or small, works on various ways of improving its organization, its processes, and its people. Most companies have a vision statement and/or mission statement and/or values statement. _But very few companies work to integrate all of these into a unified system. To do so is the point of the integration step._

A company whose values statement to become excuse-free is not integrated into its organization, processes, and people, as well as into its vision and mission statements. is like one team in a tug-of-war match in which each person on the team is tugging in a different direction. The team isn't pulling together. Any competitor with a more coordinated effort will almost surely win.

In contrast, the company that integrates the goal to become excuse-free into its entire system will work as a unit and overpower any company that pays little attention to this issue. A company with an integrated excuse-free system is a streamlined company. It is a company destined to win.

Notes and Quotes

And oftentimes excusing of a fault doth make the fault worse by the excuse.
Shakespeare: King John

CHAPTER 18

The Implementation Step: All Aboard!

Definition

Im-ple-ment v. 1. To carry into effect; to fulfill, accomplish 2, To provide the means for carrying into effect or fulfilling; to give practical effect to.

The implementation step involves getting your people to actually achieve excuse-free behavior. In the end, this is what getting results is all about. All of the understanding you've gained, and the best of your diagnostic and interventional efforts, amount to very little until the behavior is fully owned by your employees. They are the soldiers who must fight the corporate war.

Implementation is usually one of the toughest jobs when it comes to changing corporate behavior. Most leaders do a credible job of developing the concepts and understanding what needs to be done. Often they get excited about the anticipated changes. But by the time it gets to actual implementation, the whole thing falls flat. One reason for this is our mistaken belief that new behavior is something we do once or twice, and then it's learned. But human behavior doesn't change that quickly. Implementation is a never-ending process if it is to be effective.

The Five Stages of Implementation

There are five key stages to the implementation step of developing an excuse-free culture:

- **Motivation (or buy-in)**

- **Establishment of accountabilities and key indicators**

- **Benchmarking**

- **Coaching**

- **Reward and recognition**

The Distinction Between Power and Authority

Before we address each of these five stages, it is helpful to look at the distinction between power and authority. The terms are often mistakenly used interchangeably. But they differ in an important way.

Authority is the aggregate of the rights vested in, or granted to, individuals by an organization. **Power** is the ability or capacity to act on, or enforce, that authority. Usually those who have authority also have the power to enforce their authority. But not always. *Any time there is resistance to authority and the resistance succeeds, at that moment the power shifts from the authority base to the person or persons who are resisting.*

An Example

Jerry is the sales manager for an international company that distributes commercial building products. He oversees the work of 12 regional managers, each of whom supervises 6 district managers. Jerry has been granted the authority by the company to establish policy for all 72 of the people who answer to him.

Jerry established new reporting policies and regulations that took effect on January I, 1993. Specifically, each district manager was to submit a bimonthly written report to his regional manager, who in turn would submit a report to Jerry. Prior to that, reports had been required monthly. All 72 individuals resented the new policy, feeling they were too busy as it was The reports took an average of four hours to complete, and they saw it as a waste of time to do that twice a month rather than once. So they didn't do the second report each month.

Perturbed at the lack of response, Jerry restated the new policy several times throughout the year, but nothing ever changed. Whereas Jerry has the authority to fire all 72 people and start over, from a realistic point of view he can't do that. He would be without a sales force; it would he difficult to hire qualified people who were knowledgeable about the business; sales would drop drastically; and so on. The headaches would be immense. *In this situation, (1) the power has shifted from Jerry to his managers, even though Jerry still has the authority; and (2) his managers have exercised their power by not implementing his new policy.*

So What Should This Mean As It Concerns The Implementation Step?

The key to the implementation step is buy-in by employees. The key to buy-in is motivation.

Times have changed regarding motivating people in the workplace. It used to be that you could motivate people to change through the use of authority *and* power. This is no longer true. Management still has the authority to make recommendations, set policy, and decide on various matters. But the power-wielding has changed drastically from, say, 20 years ago. Management has lost much of its power to enforce policy, to hire and fire people, and to "run the show" in ways that were commonplace in the past.

Why Is This the Case?

At the dawn of the industrial age, those in authority held all the power. The collective oppression of the working people eventually caused labor to organize in reaction to the abuse of power. As a result, some of the power began shifting to the rank and file of the union. This was the first step in the movement of power away from those in positions of authority. Even so, the power gained by the working class stayed mostly in the hands of the union leaders. People in the workplace did not have personal power to change their working situations. Until about twenty years ago, the average employee worked for one company for the better part of his or her productive years. It was not uncommon for people to stay with the company that first employed them until they retired. Rarely did people jump from one company to another. And the concept of "career change" was almost unheard of.

In fact, until fairly recently there was a social and professional stigma against changing jobs. If somebody changed jobs four or five times, it was a black mark on their resume. They were considered "job hoppers." Now as you look at a resume you might wonder if someone stayed employed with a company for *too* long. There is almost a stigma against job longevity. One tends to suspect that a person who stuck to one place must have been too comfortable there, doesn't like challenge, doesn't stretch himself, may not be ambitious, probably doesn't have much diversity of experience, and so on.

The point is that in the past it was not usually in the best interests of an individual to change jobs or careers. After being with a company for X-number of years, the cut in pay that one would have to take to move to another job, including the loss of perks and benefits, prevented much movement.

But Times Have Changed

Starting with legislation in the mid-seventies—which mandated equal opportunity for all employees in a company to participate in the same retirement plan—it became more and more difficult for companies to have retirement plans for their workers. As a result, many companies dropped them.

Retirement plans were an effective method for keeping employees with the company, even if they weren't entirely happy with their jobs. With the loss of retirement plans came the loss of the golden handcuffs that held many such people in their jobs. In addition, tax laws have moved steadily in the direction of taxing all benefits, which makes the accrual of benefits to an employee less and less appealing.

Also, as companies become more sophisticated, they are moving away from seniority raises and are basing promotions and raises on merit and results. Just staying with a company does not assure promotions or additional monies as had been true in the past.

In Other Words

The social and business conditions have changed so much that there is little resemblance to what was happening 20 years ago. Middle-class America has become fairly comfortable.

It is now common practice for people to leave their jobs after four or five years. In addition, the average person changes careers three or four times in his lifetime. There is no longer sufficient financial reason for people to stay put. Most people can change jobs, or careers, with little or no loss of income and benefits.

The result is that the power base has shifted away from management toward the employees. People no longer have to stay in one job, so the threat of losing one's job has lost its power. People can usually go elsewhere to find equal or greater financial opportunity, and thus incentives have lost much of their once-magical appeal. The point is that companies can no longer motivate people to change through the traditional use of reward and punishment.

Stage One: Motivation

Motivating people in the workplace today is a new ball game. It is getting people to buy-in to change by helping them see what value the change has for them as individuals.

It is joked that the most widely listened-to radio station in our society today—one that plays non-stop at the unconscious level is station **W11-FM. What's In It-For Me!**

This frame of mind spills over into our companies in a big way. In the past, when management asked for change in behavior, the average worker was inclined to reply, "What good will this do for the company?" Today the first question is usually "What will this do for me personally?"

The point is that to motivate people in the workplace nowadays, it is important to *find out what motivates each person individually.* That is, what are the personal reasons that make changing his behavior worth his while?

Rules for the Motivation Stage

Rule #1: You can't motivate groups, only individuals.

The traditional approach to motivating people in the workplace is in the group setting. Managers stand up in front of the group and say that such and such is going to help make the company more profitable. But this approach isn't effective anymore because people aren't all that interested in what such and such will do for the company.

Since your people change for *their* reasons, not yours and not the company's, it follows that they must be worked with individually. How to do this will be covered in stage four of this chapter under "coaching".

Rule #2: Each person is motivated by different things.

We can no longer assume that everyone is motivated by the traditional incentives: job security, pay raise, and so on. Since, as we said, middle-class America is a fairly comfortable place to be today, more and more people are looking for different things from their jobs. Some people, for example, are motivated by a job that doesn't cause a lot of stress, others by never having to work more than 40 hours per week, and still others by jobs that never make demands on their time outside of normal working hours.

We can all think of countless examples of sales people who—if they stretched themselves and moved out of their comfort zones—could make considerably more money for themselves and for their companies. But they are content with the amount of money they are presently making, which leads us to rule #3.

Rule #3: Money in Itself Is not a motivation for anyone.

At least not directly. What motivates many people is what money can do. For some people money provides security; for others, freedom; for others, it's a scorecard used to meter their success; for others, it enables them to purchase "toys"; and for others it relieves the pressure of debt.

The irony is that most corporations assume that what motivates their employees is money alone. They start putting all sorts of financial incentives on the table. Most motivational programs in companies are financially based. The result is that you are only appealing to the people who are motivated by the particular form in which you are granting the money. That's one reason that the same people usually win cash-prize contests. This leaves little room for others to be motivated.

One of the most successful motivation and incentive programs we've done is to put a budget out and let each employee know what that budget was. Then we gave each of them a choice about what to do with the money if they reached their goals.

The choices included cash in combination with a trophy or plaque, specific "toys" to choose from, a shopping spree, an investment plan, etc. This allowed each employee in take the money and use it in the way that was most meaningful to him.

Then again, it's important to keep in mind that money is rarely as valuable a motivator as recognition and challenge. It is important to ascertain what type of recognition specific individuals want. Some employees are very satisfied with a nice note or letter, or just a pat on the back with private congratulations. Others want their name in lights for everyone else in the company to see.

Increasingly, research is showing us that "challenge" is becoming more and more of a personal motivator for people. Which brings up an interesting irony. Typically a company will hire people based on what they have done, not on what they may be able to do if challenged to stretch and grow. This hiring approach destines people to be unchallenged in their new jobs. Yet challenge is one of the highest motivators that we know of.

Rule #4: You must determine "who" motivates each individual.

The day is gone when we can assume that "the boss" can, or must, motivate his workers. Not everyone is motivated by supervision. Management's responsibility today is to find out whom each individual depends on for his or her motivation, and then to work with those factors. Many times we have seen people highly motivated by their spouses, so a statement like "Won't your spouse be proud of you when you accomplish such and such?" can be very effective. Sometimes people are motivated by their parents and children. We have seen many cases where people want to succeed to show their parents that they can make it on their own. In one case, we worked with a woman who was highly motivated by the fact that she wanted her eight-year-old daughter to see that she could be successful in the business world, and that business success was not just for men.

Rule #5: Stay cognizant of the fact that everything has the potential to motivate someone.

You've heard the sayings "One man's meat is another man's poison" and "Different strokes for different folks." The application of these statements here is that you never know what truly motivates each individual until you take the time to find out. For one person it may be the size of the desk, for another the location of their work station, for another the uniform they wear. It helps to refrain from imposing one's own values on what should motivate other people, and to stay open to what they prefer.

Rule #6: Whatever motivates people tends to change.

Once a person reaches his motivational objective, he will likely become motivated by whatever will help him reach his next goal. Motivation is a moving target, and managers must stay continually updated about how it is changing for each employee.

Rule #7: Motivation takes time.

Many readers will relate to what often surfaces in management seminars as the single biggest area of frustration. *How can I motivate my people?* One of the reasons for this is that motivation takes much more time than most managers ever think of spending. When you get right down to the details of how to motivate people, it requires a large investment of time spent individually with employees, trying to figure out what makes them tick, and what the right buttons are to push to keep them moving. The point of this entire section on motivation is that motivation in the workplace from now on is at the *individual* level. That is where the corporate power base now lies.

Stage Two: Establishment of Accountabilities and Key Indicators

Companies are starting to recognize and give attention to the importance of accountabilities and key indicators. We applaud this as a first step, yet more must be done in applying these concepts.

Key indicators are indicators of performance and predictors of the future. Generally, people are starting to understand the importance of defining three to five key indicators for each company. By monitoring their key indicators, an organization is in effect continually taking its own pulse. What hasn't yet been accomplished, however, is applying the same concept to each employee. The goal is to have three to five key indicators for each person that serve as his or her accountabilities.

Traditionally, accountabilities have been tied directly into the vision and mission statements, and have therefore been task-based. Emphasis has been on attaining sales quotas, getting reports in on time, achieving less than five percent error in processing paperwork, and so on.

Most companies today are still following this same pattern of building accountabilities around the vision and mission statements. This approach will not work if the goal is to become excuse-free. Corporations must begin to place more emphasis on their values statement than on their vision and mission statements The fast-changing conditions of the marketplace require that it is more important to have the right behavior than the right mission. People with the right behavior will automatically develop the right mission.

By the same token, companies that begin to tie their employees' accountabilities and key indicators into employee behavior will discover two distinct benefits. First, they will be changing and enhancing employee behavior, which is the goal of accountabilities in the first place. Second, they will not limit employee performance by putting a ceiling on whatever the task at hand is, as tends to happen when accountabilities are measured by task accomplishment. Instead, workers will have the flexibility to adapt as needed, as long as the emphasis is on their excuse-free behavior. The point is that behavior-based accountabilities keep employees more attuned to changing with a fast-changing market.

We're saying that accountabilities and key indicators must be tied into the values statement—specifically, into the values statement to become excuse-free. This values statement is behavior-based rather than task-based, and therefore builds in more latitude and more flexibility for responding to market conditions.

The role of accountabilities in the development of an excuse-free culture is such an enormous topic that we can barely mention it here. Future books and newsletters will devote considerable time to this critical element of the success formula. For now, your task is to look at the accountabilities and key indicators that you have and see if they are behavior-based or task-based. Once this is determined, we'll help you move forward from there.

Stage Three: Benchmarking

Benchmarking is about the need for measurement. If you want to improve something, you must measure it. What benchmarking does is set a starting point and a methodology for measuring the progress of any change effort you wish to undertake.

The tool we recommend for benchmarking is the same one used for the diagnosis, namely, the 360° survey. Whereas the questions will be different, what will be the same is that they will be qualitative rather than quantitative, since what must be measured is behavior, not task completion. Benchmarking is helpful for this because it allows the accumulation of a number of opinions from different perspectives. As you do the benchmarking, you are also looking to make sure that the weaknesses and difficulties that show up are tied into the accountabilities and key indicators. The two processes go hand in hand.

This is similar to what we mentioned in Chapter 14 about training and development programs. The practice of training people without pre- and post-measurements often amounts to a waste of resources because there is no way to know for certain whether or not any change occurred. So with accountabilities: In order to know whether or not the factors for which a person is held accountable have been achieved, those factors must be periodically measured. Otherwise, too much is left to subjective interpretation. And this becomes a breeding ground for conflict, passing of responsibilities, projection of blame, and all the other excuse-related behaviors.

Stage Four: Coaching

Coaching is for individuals, not teams. This relates back to rule #1 under the motivation stage. You can't motivate groups, only individuals.

Yet this is precisely what makes the coaching step undoubtably the most difficult of all. Finding the time to properly coach individuals is a very difficult challenge for managers and leaders today, given the flattening of management structures and an increase in the ratio of employees to managers. Part of the reason for the difficulty, however, is that coaching sessions are too often based on "telling" rather than on facilitation.

The point of coaching is not to have a two-hour sit down session every week so that the manager can tell the employee what to do. It is, rather, a process whereby an employee learns how to coach himself to reach his own answers, solutions, and directions under the mentorship of his manager. Again, this could take volumes to cover in detail, which we promise to do in other books and newsletters. There are a few elements, however, that can be stressed here.

- **Coaching sessions must be regularly planned and executed, preferably no less often than twice a month, and ideally once a week.**

- **Coaching sessions should always have a predetermined agenda, with no surprises.**

- **The manager should be asking questions, and the employee should be doing most of the talking.**

- **The focus of the coaching session should be on behavior, not tasks.**

- **Coaching sessions should be limited to a certain length of time. Twenty to thirty minutes is a good average. In the first coaching session, employee and employer will struggle to hold the time to that limit. However, by insisting that the time be held to a specific limit, eventually both will become more focused and better prepared, and you will find that it takes less time than at first. This awareness is critical because our experience indicates that managers get away from coaching their people mainly because of time constraints. Yet the issue of time constraints doesn't need to be a major concern. A manager with eight employees reporting directly to him surely should be able to find four hours a week to properly coach his people. What tends to happen, however, is that the four hours expand to ten, and neither employee nor employer sees a lot of value in the process because there is too much "telling" and not enough questioning and development.**

Stage Five: Reward and Recognition

When a company is successful in implementing excuse-free behavior, a celebration is clearly in order. Keeping in mind that the celebration may have to be individually tailored, let's not forget that implementation without some type of reward and recognition is like winning an Olympic marathon and not getting a gold medal. The reward is necessary to complete the task of helping people reach their goal of "what's in it for me," which is the motivation that began the entire process of change.

And Last

In the end, the power to implement excuse-free behavior rests with the employees and not with management. We repeatedly hear employees crying out for help to become more empowered. This management system—*Let's Get Results, Not Excuses*—and, in particular, this implementation step, is empowerment in the fullest sense of the word. The goal of everyone in any organization should be to empower the employees in that organization. That goal can finally be reached through excuse-free behavior. The implementation step is virtually impossible without successful high-level communications. All five steps are critically tied to the concept of good communication. Again, however, to spell out the details of a communication style that will best accomplish these various steps would far exceed the space limitations of this book. Yet committed as we are to the cause of giving you a total, airtight package for eliminating excuses from your workplace, we will soon publish other needed information.

Notes and Quotes

Where the heart is willing, it will find a thousand ways, but where the heart is weak, it will find a thousand excuses.

Anonymous

CHAPTER 17

In Conclusion

We said in the preface that the subject of excuse-making is far too big a topic to cover in a single work, and that this book would be at most an introduction to the problems that result from excuses in the workplace. As promised, much more information will follow on this new management approach.

Nevertheless, we are faced at this point with the question, "How do we end a book about a subject that we have just begun to explore?" Obviously, it wouldn't be practical, nor does space allow, for a review of every point made throughout the book. Still, there are certain signposts that do mark the trail of where this book has taken you.

Our hope is that a review of these main points will help solidify the basics of how excuses operate in our organizations, and the many dangers that they pose.

1. People Make Excuses to Protect Themselves

There is nothing inherently devious or immoral about excuse-making. Everybody does it on occasion As the eye blinks reflexively when an object moves suddenly toward it, excuse-making is an instinctive, unconscious, automatic response to protect oneself in the face of real or perceived criticism, blame, or failure.

While in some ways excuses are like lies and rationalizations, excuses are unique in that they are more socially acceptable, and therefore are more generalized and pervasive. As a self-protective mechanism, excuse-making is by and large a culturally sanctioned way of behaving, whereas lying and rationalizing are more typically viewed as personality weaknesses and character flaws.

In the majority of people, excuse-making is well practiced by the age of four. In corporate America, this four-year-old behavior resurfaces often and expresses itself extensively because of the many situations in our organizations and processes that tend to invite, allow, encourage, and even "force" self-protection.

2. Excuses and Reasons Are Very Difficult to Distinguish from One Another

Excuses and reasons both function to explain why we did or didn't do something on those occasions when we feel that our behavior needs to be justified. The differences between excuses and reasons are very subtle, so much so that it is nearly impossible to distinguish one from the other. At first glance, this presents itself as a dilemma. On the one hand, we must eliminate excuses from the workplace, but on the other, we usually can't determine the difference between an excuse and a good reason. How, then, do we go about getting rid of excuses?

The secret is to understand that excuses happen _after the fact,_ when people are put in positions where they might face the possibility of criticism, blame, or failure. Excuse-making is automatic and self-protective, so dealing with excuses after the fact is already too late. The excuse-making process cannot very well be reversed at that point. Instead, excuses must be headed off _before the fact_ by properly setting things up so that people are not put in situations where they need to defend themselves.

3. Excuses Are Dangerous to Our Companies: They Never Exist Alone

Wherever there are excuses, there are also many other problems infecting corporate America. Excuses and other corporate problems always appear together. The symptoms include reactive thinking, denial of responsibility, projection of blame, victimization, pessimism, procrastination, helplessness, can't-do attitudes, entitlement, incompetence, fearfulness, complacency, lack of pride in workmanship, externalization, conflict, poor teamwork, avoidance of issues, and self-deceit. Excuse-making "goes with" every one of these behavior problems. Their relationship is systemic in that the chronic problems facing our organizations and excuse-making are mutually coexistent—one cannot exist without the other.

4. When You Get Rid of Excuses, All the Other Problems Go Away

This is what makes our approach to management truly revolutionary. Excuse-making is the one common denominator of every management problem. *Get rid of excuses and you get rid of all the other problems. That's why, if you want results, you must get rid of excuses!*

This is in striking contrast to other, more traditional approaches to corporate problem solving. Typically the person in charge has a list of organizational problems.

Perhaps those problems are obvious, or maybe they turned up in a traditional audit. Either way, the next step is to go out and hire one consulting or training firm to address one problem, another firm to address the next problem, and so on, one problem at a time.

Usually each consulting and training project is totally independent of the others. As a result, there is little if any harmony of purpose; little if any regard for sequence and timing; little if any measurement to determine what is and isn't working. This is not to mention the fact that the problem being addressed may be more of a symptom than the real, underlying problem. None of this is true about developing an excuse-free culture. *One stone kills all the birds at the same time.*

Harmony of purpose, sequence and timing, measurement and adjustment, and addressing the real problem—these are all givens when you work to create an excuse-free culture. **When you get rid of excuses, all the other problems go away.**

5. The Best Way to Get Rid of Excuses Is to Create an Extraordinary Organization with Extraordinary Processes

In order to get people to stop making excuses in the workplace, you must first get rid of the reasons that people make excuses. You do this by creating an extraordinary organization with extraordinary processes. The consequence is that you then get extraordinary performance out of ordinary people. **In other words. you get results. Not excuses!**

6. Step One in Creating an Extraordinary Organization with Extraordinary Processes Is to Make Sure That You Have the Right People in Leadership Positions

Leaders, managers, and administrators don't perform the same functions. Administrators administer past policy; managers manage current conditions; leaders lead by showing the way, introducing, and going first. Leadership is, by definition, proactive, creative, empowered, optimistic—in short, excuse-free.

The leadership that your company needs in the quest to become number one does not happen by chance. It is the result of an aggressively pursued course of action where effective leaders are sought out, hired, promoted, rewarded, developed, and trained. Whether they come from the ranks of management or non-management, whether from inside the company or outside, whether they are experienced or not, the point is that you must have the right leaders in order to develop an excuse-free culture and, consequently, to get the results that you really want.

7. It Gets Easier from There

Ours is a management system based on the importance of changing **behavior.** That is a unique approach. It moves the focus from what people do to how they do it to the standards of conduct. In other words, it moves the focus from vision and mission statements to values statements—in particular, to the values statement of becoming and remaining excuse-free.

Once you are committed to the values statement of having an excuse-free culture, then you diagnose where the excuse-making virus is at work in your company. Next you intervene by getting your leaders in place to lead your people into excuse-free behavior. This enables you to integrate your vision, mission, and values statements in order to create an extraordinary organization with extraordinary processes. It's smooth sailing the rest of the way. Implementing the system—benchmarking, establishing accountabilities and key indicators, measuring behaviors by use of 360-degree audits, motivating, coaching, rewarding—is a relatively straightforward process once you understand that the key to corporate success is excuse-free behavior in your people.

A Final Note

In spite of all the recent negativity about American business, the time has come when some credit is due. Though for years our status in the world marketplace fell steadily, we are coming back. The message of the doomsayers who continue to beat the drum that American business is losing the race is beginning to sound old. The sky is not falling, and it is not time to run for the hills.

But we still have our share of problems. One of those problems—in fact, *the biggest single problem facing our companies today*—is the problem of excuse-making in the workplace. The problem is not that we've ignored it or denied it or pretended that it wasn't there. *The problem is that we haven't before recognized excuse-making as the huge problem that it is.*

But now we do recognize it. And because we do, the qualities of the American people that made this country and its companies number one before will make us number one again. *The enemy is known, and that enemy is excuse-making. When excuses go, results happen. And getting results is what being number one is all about!*

Notes and Quotes

Ten of the most commonly used excuses in the workplace:
1. That's the way we've always done it.
2. I didn't know you were in a hurry for it.
3. That's not in my department.
4. No one told me to go ahead.
5. I'm waiting for an okay.
6. I didn't think it would make any difference.
7. That's his job, not mine.
8. Wait till the boss comes back and ask him.
9. I'm so busy. I forgot.
10. I just work here; I'm not paid to make decisions.

Unknown

BIBLIOGRAPHY

Bardwick, Judith M. *Danger in the Comfort Zone.* New York, NY: AMACOM, a division of American Management Association, 1991.

Bennis, Warren. *On Becoming a Leader.* Reading, MA: Addison-Wesley Publishing Company, 1989.

Bliss, Edwin C. *Doing It Now: A Twelve-Step Program for Curing Procrastination and Achieving Your Goals.* New York, NY: Scribner, 1983.

Burke, Jane B. Procrastination: *Why You Do It, What to Do About It.* Reading, MA: Addison-Wesley Publishing Company, 1983

Caldwell, John. *Excuses, Excuses: How to Get Out of Practically Everything.* New York, NY: Crowell, 1981.

Colson, Chuck, and Jack Eckerd. *Why America Doesn't Work.* Dallas, TX: Word Publishing, 1991.

Connors, Roger. *The Oz Principle.* Englewood Cliffs, NJ: Prentice-Hall, 1993.

Covey, Stephen R. *The 7 Habits of Highly Effective People.* New York, NY: Simon and Schuster, 1989.

Iacocca, Lee. *Iacocc: An Autobiography*. With William Novak. New York, NY: Bantam Books, Inc.. 1984.

Johnson, Linda Carlson *Responsibility*. New York, NY: Rosen Publishing Group, 1990.

Mead, Lawrence M *Beyond Entitlement: The Social Obligations of Citizenship*. New York, NY: Free Press, 1986.

Monks, Robert. *Power and Accountability*. New York, NY: Harper Business, 1991.

O'toole, James. *Making America Work: Productivity and Responsibility*. New York, NY. Continum, 1981.

Rodgers, T.J., William Taylor, and Rick Foreman. *No Excuses Management*. New York, NY: Doubleday, 1992.

Ryan, Kathleen D., and Daniel K. Oestreich. *Driving Fear Out of the Workplace*. San Francisco: Jossey-Bass Publishers, 1991.

Scherkenbach, William W. *The Deming Route to Quality and Productivity*. Washington, DC: CEE Press Books, 1992.

Stevenson, Burton Ebert *The Home Book of Verse*. New York-Chicago-San Francisco: Holt, Reinhart, Winston, 1953.

Wahlroos, Sven *Excuses*. New York, NY: MacMillan Publishing Company, Inc" 1981.

Walton, Mary. *The Deming Management Method*. New York, NY: Perigee Books, 1986.

Seminar Notes

Seminar Notes

Seminar Notes

Seminar Notes

Seminar Notes

Fell's

Official Know-It-All Guide™

Check out these exciting titles in our Know-It-All™ series, available at your favorite bookstore:

- ❏ Fell's Official Know-It-All™ Guide: **Advanced Hypnotism**
- ❏ Fell's Official Know-It-All™ Guide: **Advanced Magic**
- ❏ Fell's Official Know-It-All™ Guide: **The Art of Traveling Extravagantly & Nearly Free**
- ❏ Fell's Official Know-It-All™ Guide: **Budget Weddings**
- ❏ Fell's Official Know-It-All™ Guide: **Career Planning**
- ❏ Fell's Official Know-It-All™ Guide: **Contract Bridge**
- ❏ Fell's Official Know-It-All™ Guide: **Coins 2003**
- ❏ Fell's Official Know-It-All™ Guide: **Cruises**
- ❏ Fell's Official Know-It-All™ Guide: **Defensive Divorce**
- ❏ Fell's Official Know-It-All™ Guide: **Dreams**
- ❏ Fell's Official Know-It-All™ Guide: **Easy Entertaining**
- ❏ Fell's Official Know-It-All™ Guide: **ESP Power**
- ❏ Fell's Official Know-It-All™ Guide: **Getting Rich & Staying Rich**
- ❏ Fell's Official Know-It-All™ Guide: **Health & Wellness**
- ❏ Fell's Official Know-It-All™ Guide: **Magic For Beginners**
- ❏ Fell's Official Know-It-All™ Guide: **Money Management for College Students**
- ❏ Fell's Official Know-It-All™ Guide: **Mortgage Maze**
- ❏ Fell's Official Know-It-All™ Guide: **No Bull Selling**
- ❏ Fell's Official Know-It-All™ Guide: **Nutrition For a New America**
- ❏ Fell's Official Know-It-All™ Guide: **Online Investing**
- ❏ Fell's Official Know-It-All™ Guide: **Palm Reading**
- ❏ Fell's Official Know-It-All™ Guide: **Relationship Selling**
- ❏ Fell's Official Know-It-All™ Guide: **Secrets of Mind Power**
- ❏ Fell's Official Know-It-All™ Guide: **So, You Want to Be a Teacher?**
- ❏ Fell's Official Know-It-All™ Guide: **Super Power Memory**
- ❏ Fell's Official Know-It-All™ Guide: **Ultimate Beauty Recipes**
- ❏ Fell's Official Know-It-All™ Guide: **Wedding Planner**
- ❏ Fell's Official Know-It-All™ Guide: **Wisdom in the Office**